WE LOVE
QUINOA

First published in the UK in 2016 by
Apple Press
74–77 White Lion Street
London N1 9PF
United Kingdom

www.apple-press.com

ISBN 9781845436360

Printed in China by Shanghai Offset Printing Products Ltd
9 8 7 6 5 4 3 2 1

This book was conceived, designed and produced by
Quantum Books Limited
6 Blundell Street
London N7 9BH
United Kingdom

Publisher: Kerry Enzor
Project Editors: Charlotte Frost and Lucy Kingett
Editorial Assistant: Emma Harverson
Production Manager: Zarni Win
Designer: Simon Goggin
Food Styling by Jassy Davis
Photography by Simon Pask

QUMWLQH

WE LOVE
QUINOA

Over 100 Delicious & Healthy Hand-Picked Recipes

KAREN S. BURNS-BOOTH

CAROLYN COPE

JASSY DAVIS

KRISTINA SLOGGETT

JACKIE SOBON

APPLE

CONTENTS

Meet the Bloggers   8

WHY WE LOVE QUINOA

10 Ways to Eat More Quinoa   14

Cooking Quinoa is Easy!   18

BREAKFAST & BRUNCH

Cacao Quinoa Protein Shake   22

Toasted Coconut and Quinoa
   Breakfast Pudding   24

Pecan Quinoa Porridge   28

Vanilla Cardamom Quinoa Granola   32

Quinoa Pancakes with Spiced Strawberry
   Compote and Yoghurt   36

Quinoa Crêpes with Berries and Ricotta   38

Quinoa Waffles with Berry Compote   40

Quinoa, Feta Cheese and Spinach
   Breakfast Muffins   44

Quinoa, Cheddar and Chive Mini Frittatas   48

Quinoa Chickpea Scramble Burrito   51

SNACKS & APPETIZERS

Quinoa-Dusted Tortilla Chips with
   Artichoke and Rocket Dip   56

Smoky Aubergine and Quinoa Dip   58

Pumped-Up Five-Layer Quinoa Dip   60

Cheesy Hot Sauce Quinoa Bites   62

Puffed Quinoa Bhelpuri   66

Sweet Potato Quinoa Kibbeh   68

Quinoa Lettuce Wraps   70

Quinoa-Coated Fish Finger Sandwich   74

Grilled Veggie and Quinoa Summer Rolls
   with Cajun Tahini Sauce   76

Quinoa Crab Cakes   78

22

24

32

36

48

51

58

66

78

MAIN COURSES

Quinoa Pizza with Blue Cheese and Aubergine   82

Sprouted Quinoa Chirashi Sushi Bowl   86

Sprouted Quinoa and Salmon Temaki Sushi   89

Quinoa Bean Burger with Basil Aïoli   92

Spicy Peanut Veggie Stew with Quinoa Dumplings   96

Vegetable Paella-Style Quinoa   98

Chipotle Sweet Potato Quinoa Enchiladas   102

Black Bean, Quinoa and Vegetable Chilli   104

Risotto-Style Quinoa with Caramelized Onions and Mushrooms   106

Smoky Spanish Quinoa with Chicken and Chorizo   110

Lamb and Quinoa Meatballs   112

SOUPS, SALADS & SIDES

Roasted Cauliflower Quinoa Soup   118

Curry Squash Quinoa Bisque with Coconut Cream   120

Quinoa Couscous with Blood Oranges and Burrata   122

Quinoa Kisir with Pomegranate and Walnuts   126

Summer Quinoa Salad with Grapefruit and Tahini Dressing   128

Fruity Quinoa Tabbouleh with Feta Cheese   130

Beetroot and Carrot Quinoa Cakes with Cumin Yoghurt Sauce   134

Thai-Style Crab, Pomelo and Quinoa Salad   136

Roasted Winter Vegetable, Quinoa and Wild Rice Salad   138

BAKES & DESSERTS

Fluffy and Fruity Quinoa Scones   142

Power Boost Snickerdoodles   146

Chocolate Peanut Butter Bars   148

Rich and Fudgy Quinoa Brownies   152

Quinoa Cinnamon Power Bites   154

Blueberry Pistachio Quinoa Parfait with Quinoa Praline   158

Spiced Cashew 'Cheesecake' with Red Quinoa Crust   162

Iced Orange, Semolina and Quinoa Layer Cake   164

Apple Crumble with Quinoa Topping   166

Multiseed and Quinoa Bread   170

Index   172

Recipe List by Blogger   175

Acknowledgements   176

KEY TO SYMBOLS

(V) **VEGETARIAN**

(VG) **VEGAN (AND VEGETARIAN)**

(DF) **DAIRY-FREE**

(GF) **GLUTEN-FREE**

(WF) **WHEAT-FREE**

Vegetarian and vegan recipes are tagged at the top of the pages showing main recipes.

96

102

110

120

136

138

142

146

162

MEET THE BLOGGERS

KAREN S. BURNS-BOOTH is a professional recipe writer and food stylist who splits her time between the UK and France. In addition to writing for her own site, **Lavender and Lovage,** she regularly contributes to a variety of print publications and creates recipes for major brands in the UK and Europe.

CAROLYN COPE is a food and lifestyle writer and the voice behind the popular blog **Umami Girl,** where the world is equal parts eat-to-live and live-to-eat. An avid traveller, musician and yogi, she is based in greater New York City, USA.

JASSY DAVIS is a London-based recipe writer for organic vegetable company Abel & Cole and a professional food stylist. Her recipes in this book are inspired by Asian flavours and world food. Her blog is **Gin and Crumpets.**

KRISTINA SLOGGETT is a vegan health-food writer and recipe developer. Her blog **spabettie** focuses on plant-based recipes with vibrant colours and bright flavours for the vegan community. She currently lives in Portland, Oregon, USA.

JACKIE SOBON is both the chef and the photographer behind the blog **Vegan Yack Attack;** cooking food and taking beautiful pictures is her passion and 'Camera Eats First' is her motto. Her work has been featured on websites, on news outlets and in magazines around the globe. Jackie is based in California, USA.

WHY WE LOVE QUINOA

QUINOA (PRONOUNCED 'KEEN-WAH') IS A FANTASTIC 'SUPER' FOOD THAT IS COMPATIBLE WITH GLUTEN-FREE, VEGAN AND VEGETARIAN DIETS.

QUINOA IS ANCIENT

Quinoa has been feeding humans for thousands of years. People in the Andean region of South America – Peru, Bolivia, Ecuador, Chile and Colombia – first began domesticating the crop between 3,000 and 4,000 years ago (see page 12). All crops change over time, but thanks to the maintenance of nature-friendly ancestral farming practices by the people of the Andes, quinoa continues to exist in its natural state. That's great news from both a global health perspective and a culinary one, because quinoa offers a mild but unique flavour profile that cooks are lucky to have. Quinoa is being touted as a reliable contribution to global food security. It's a high-quality food source that thrives in challenging climates, and it has the potential to help feed the world's growing population in years to come. On this basis, the United Nations even designated 2013 the international year of quinoa.

IN THE KITCHEN

Quinoa is often included in discussions about whole grains because it shares a lot of their culinary properties and proclivities. Technically, though, it's a pseudo-grain – an edible seed related to spinach, beetroot and amaranth.

Quinoa grows in a rainbow of colours, but by far the most common varieties are white, red and black. You can use them interchangeably, especially if it's difficult to find the variety called for in a recipe. Here's what you need to know about each colour: white quinoa is a little softer than the other varieties after cooking, making it especially great for porridges, risotto- and paella-style dishes and baked goods; red and black quinoa stay a little crunchier and the individual seeds remain more separate when cooked, so they're nice in salads, mixed with whole grains for textural variety or anywhere you'd like to advertise quinoa's presence.

Due to its impressive versatility, quinoa is a great contribution to both savoury and sweet dishes, from breakfast to dessert with snacks in between. As you'll see from the recipes in this book, quinoa also integrates well into dishes with a wide

Quinoa comes in a range of different colours. The most commonly sold are red, black and white, which can be bought separately but are also sold as a tricolour mix (pictured here).

variety of cultural origins. Though initially cultivated only in the Americas, quinoa has spread across the globe, in part because cooks the world over understand its potential to enliven traditional dishes. As well as cooking the quinoa you can also puff it (see page 66), sprout it (see page 91) or use it in its flour form.

Quinoa flour is a flavourful and versatile ingredient that can be used to replace wheat flour in a range of baked goods and other recipes. It is increasingly available in stops as well as being easy to make at home.

To make quinoa flour, rinse the grains and then toast them until they are completely dry. Place the toasted quinoa into a high-speed blender or a spice grinder and process it until finely ground.

Try substituting plain flour with quinoa flour in muffin and pancake recipes; using a spoonful to thicken a soup or stew; or adding a scoop to a smoothie for an extra dose of protein and fibre.

QUINOA IS GOOD FOR YOU

Quinoa's tiny size and mild taste belie its status as a nutritional powerhouse. It is a rare, plant-based source of complete protein, meaning it contains all nine of the amino acids that our bodies need but cannot produce on their own. That's why you'll often hear quinoa referred to as a high-quality protein source.

In addition to protein, quinoa boasts a substantial amount of dietary fibre, lots of antioxidants, plenty of iron, potassium, magnesium and vitamins B, K and E. And that's just what we know today. Since quinoa is a whole food with ancient roots, it's safe to assume that its benefits far outpace our current nutritional understanding. We can simply eat it and reap more advantages than we know.

And if that isn't enough, quinoa is also gluten-free. Because it can mimic ingredients such as flour, breadcrumbs and grains in many recipes, quinoa is a great gift to those with gluten allergies and intolerance to wheat and other processed grains.

WHERE QUINOA COMES FROM

Unlike many popular food sources today, quinoa is still grown predominantly by small farmers and associations. For that reason, and because it provides a high-quality alternative to less-efficient forms of protein derived from meat and fish, its proliferation tends to be a good thing for the environment.

Quinoa thrives in cool, arid climates where many other crops can't live. Today, the majority of quinoa still comes from the mountains and coastal valleys of Peru, Ecuador, Chile and Bolivia. But as its popularity and profit potential increase, cultivation has spread to many parts of the world. You'll now find quinoa growing across Europe – from the Netherlands, to the UK, to Italy. In the USA, quinoa grows in Colorado and Nevada, and in Canada you'll find it in Ontario.

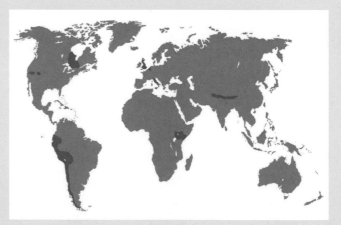

Showing its potential to feed people across the globe, quinoa has also been grown successfully in parts of Kenya and in the Himalayas. This chart shows areas of blue where quinoa is commonly grown.

5 GREAT FLAVOUR COMBINATIONS

Quinoa's adaptable flavour profile works well with a vast range of ingredient combinations. Here are five groups of complementary flavours to spark your creativity while standing in the kitchen, quinoa in hand.

- Quinoa + Garlic + Prawn + Feta Cheese + Dill
- Quinoa + Strawberries + Swiss Chard + Pistachios + Mint
- Quinoa + Almond Milk + Cinnamon + Nutmeg + Maple Syrup
- Quinoa + Shiitake Mushrooms + Shallots + White Wine + Soya Sauce
- Quinoa + Tomatoes + Cucumber + Yellow Pepper + Red Onion

10 WAYS TO EAT MORE QUINOA

1 MORNINGS

Supercharge your mornings by adding quinoa. What better way to start the day? Toast some quinoa for added crunch in your granola, as with the Vanilla Cardamom Quinoa Granola on page 32. Or, for a creamy and nourishing start to the day, give your porridge a makeover by trying the Pecan Quinoa Porridge on page 28.

2 EGG DISHES

Give your egg dishes an extra protein boost with a generous helping of quinoa, as with the Quinoa, Cheddar and Chive Mini Frittatas on page 48. The extra fibre and protein will help you get through busy days.

3 SALADS

Are you tired of predictable salads? Spruce them up by adding quinoa and you'll see exactly how versatile the ancient grain is. Make the most of summer with a sweet-and-savoury fix, as in the Summer Quinoa Salad with Grapefruit Tahini Dressing on page 128. Or try the sensational Thai-Style Crab, Pomelo and Quinoa Salad on page 136.

4 SPORTS PREP/RECOVERY

Fuel your body before or after a workout with quinoa's proteins and complex carbohydrates. Feel better prepared and recover more quickly with the added nutrients and tasty crunch of quinoa. You can't beat portable snacks, like the Quinoa Cinnamon Power Bites on page 154.

5 BURGERS (MEAT OR VEGGIE)

For a healthy and delicious crowd pleaser, why not mix a generous scoop of cooked quinoa into your burger patties? Enjoy the added fibre and lighter texture, like the Quinoa Bean Burger with Basil Aïoli on page 92.

6 INSTEAD OF RICE

Discover the versatility of quinoa when you swap rice for quinoa in your favourite dishes. Stay full and nourished for longer with the Risotto-Style Quinoa with Caramelized Onions and Mushrooms on page 106. Or use quinoa in ways you'd never considered before, as with the Sprouted Quinoa and Salmon Temaki Sushi on page 89.

7 SOUPS AND STEWS

This is one of the easiest ways to include more quinoa in your diet. Swap potatoes or noodles for quinoa to make a satisfying addition to hearty soups and stews. Toss in a handful of rinsed, drained quinoa to vegetable soups, like the Roasted Cauliflower Quinoa Soup on page 118. Quinoa dumplings make a great winter warmer, as with the Spicy Peanut Veggie Stew with Quinoa Dumplings on page 96.

 **BREADING: FISH, MEAT & VEG**

Breading baked meats, fish and vegetables in quinoa can quickly transform a 'tasty' dinner into a 'tasty and healthy' dinner. Give comfort foods a crispy and delicious coating, and try the Quinoa-Coated Fish Finger Sandwich on page 74.

9 CAKES AND BISCUITS

Let go of the guilt and satisfy your sweet tooth with the protein-rich goodness of quinoa. Enjoy something sweet and filling with extra vitamins, like the Rich and Fudgy Quinoa Brownies on page 152. Or, for a one-stop boost of energy and nutrients combined with a traditional cookie recipe, try the American-style Power Boost Snickerdoodles on page 146.

 **MILKSHAKES AND BABY FOOD**

Quinoa can be enjoyed by the whole family! Soft, small and generally not an allergen, quinoa is considered a good choice as an early solid food for your baby. Enliven creamy milkshakes, purées and cereals with the added vitamins and fibre of quinoa. Please consult with your doctor first to determine what is best for your baby.

Quinoa is incredibly versatile and can be used in sweet and savoury dishes alike. It works wonderfully well as a substitute for rice and noodles. Try the recipe for Grilled Veggie and Quinoa Summer Rolls with Cajun Tahini Sauce on page 76 – delicious!

COOKING QUINOA IS EASY!

Cooking quinoa is super simple – in many ways it's a very similar process to cooking rice. You can get a creamy consistency or fluffy, dry grains.

RINSE AND REPEAT: If you've ever tried quinoa and not liked the taste, it's probably because it wasn't rinsed properly. The first step in preparing quinoa is an important one: place it in a fine-mesh sieve and rinse it very well under lukewarm water. Continue until the water runs clear, moving the quinoa around in the sieve with your hand. Then rinse a little more. This washes away quinoa's natural coating, called saponin, which protects it from predators as it grows, but needs to be removed before cooking. Some packaged quinoa has been pre-rinsed, but it's best to do it at home anyway just to be sure.

TOAST IF YOU LIKE: Quinoa has a fairly mild flavour profile, which makes it highly versatile. But in certain dishes you'll want to bring out its full potential for nuttiness. That's when you'll take the additional step of toasting rinsed and drained quinoa in a dry pan, or in a tablespoon of oil or butter, before adding cooking liquid. Place the pan over a medium-high heat, pour in the quinoa and cook, stirring frequently, until the quinoa is dry, smells toasty and begins to take on a hint of colour. Then proceed with the recipe.

SIMMER AWAY: A good rule of thumb for the proper amount of cooking liquid is two parts liquid to one part quinoa. A particular recipe may vary this ratio slightly – a bit less for a salad, a bit more for a porridge. But if you're freewheeling in the kitchen and you stick to this ratio, the results will never be too far from perfect. Quinoa happily takes on the

FREEZING QUINOA

Even though quinoa is quick to prepare from scratch, some days you just don't have the time. That's when it's wonderful to be able to reach into the freezer for an individual portion of cooked quinoa that, once defrosted, will be virtually indistinguishable from the fresh stuff.

When you're making a pot of quinoa, double or triple the recipe. Let the leftovers cool completely. (Speed this process by spreading it out on a rimmed baking tray if you like.) Then measure out individual portions – 180–360 g (6¼–12½ oz.) works nicely – and place into zip-lock bags or small, lidded containers. For reference, a standard sized sandwich bag holds about 360 g (12½ oz.).

Squeeze any air out of the bags and place in the freezer, inside a larger freezer-safe bag if you like. Freeze for up to 3 months. When ready to use, simply defrost on the counter or place in a bowl in the microwave for about a minute.

flavours of the liquid in which it's cooked, and there's virtually no limit to the options you can try. Water works just fine in most cases. Swirl in a little fine sea salt and a knob of butter or drizzle of oil if you like. Or feel free to get fancy. A richly flavoured stock will shine in a savoury dish. Dairy and non-dairy milks add creaminess to porridge, while juices like apple and orange brighten up sweet salads and desserts. Add a splash of wine when it feels right, and experiment with mixing liquids.

With your quinoa in the saucepan, pour in the liquid and bring to a boil over a high heat. Cover the saucepan tightly and reduce the heat to maintain a gentle simmer. Quinoa generally cooks in about 15 minutes and is finished when it's just tender and you can see a little curlicue in each piece.

RESTING & FLUFFING: After cooking, let the quinoa rest off the heat in the lidded saucepan for 10 minutes. For the very best results, drape a clean tea towel just over the surface of the quinoa and replace the lid on the top. The towel will absorb any excess moisture and save the quinoa from the slightest hint of sogginess.

After 10 minutes, remove the lid and tea towel and use a fork to fluff the quinoa, gently separating the pieces. The quinoa is now ready to eat plain or mix into a recipe.

PREPARING AHEAD: A pot of simply cooked quinoa in the fridge is a valuable resource during busy times. It keeps well, tightly covered, for up to a week – although with all the enticing ways to use it, it's unlikely to last that long. Cooked quinoa also freezes beautifully (see box on page 18).

NOTES ON OTHER INGREDIENTS

EGGS: The recipes throughout this book use medium, free-range eggs. Medium eggs typically weigh 57 g (2 oz.), the equivalent of 3¼ tablespoons. Free-range eggs mean that the hens that laid them are uncaged and have some access to outdoor space, hopefully allowing them to engage in natural behaviours.

BUTTER: When you recreate these recipes, the butter used should be unsalted unless otherwise stated in the recipe. This allows you to control the salt levels in your cooking and customize it to your taste by adding as much or as little salt as you like. Salted butter can also mask other flavours, therefore downplaying the taste of the rest of your ingredients.

SALT: All recipes in the book use table salt unless noted. The grains of table salt are finer and more uniform than other types of salt and this allows them to be more evenly distributed.

SUGAR: Unless otherwise specified, granulated white sugar is the sugar used in all recipes. Granulated sugar gives the best baking results as the larger crystals allow more air into the mixture, therefore creating a lighter texture.

FRUITS AND VEGETABLES: For fruits and vegetables that vary in size (e.g. potatoes, onions, carrots), please assume that they are medium-sized unless otherwise stated in the recipe.

WHEN A RECIPE CALLS FOR UNCOOKED QUINOA, ALWAYS RINSE IT BEFORE USE.

BREAKFAST & BRUNCH

CACAO QUINOA PROTEIN SHAKE

TOASTED COCONUT AND QUINOA BREAKFAST PUDDING

PECAN QUINOA PORRIDGE

VANILLA CARDAMOM QUINOA GRANOLA

QUINOA PANCAKES WITH SPICED STRAWBERRY COMPOTE AND YOGHURT

QUINOA CRÊPES WITH BERRIES AND RICOTTA

QUINOA WAFFLES WITH BERRY COMPOTE

QUINOA, FETA CHEESE AND SPINACH BREAKFAST MUFFINS

QUINOA, CHEDDAR AND CHIVE MINI FRITTATAS

QUINOA CHICKPEA SCRAMBLE BURRITO

Recipe on page 38

CACAO QUINOA PROTEIN SHAKE

MAKES	2
PREP	5 minutes

YOU WILL NEED

2 large frozen bananas, broken into pieces

3 tablespoons cacao nibs, plus extra for garnish

3 tablespoons cacao powder

3 Medjool dates, pitted and chopped

2 tablespoons quinoa flour

1 tablespoon almond butter

1 teaspoon maca powder

240 ml (8½ fl oz.) non-dairy milk

1 teaspoon agave nectar (optional)

ice (optional)

FREE FROM
DAIRY, GLUTEN & WHEAT

WHEN YOU WORK HARD, YOU NEED TO REPLENISH YOURSELF IN THE RIGHT WAY. QUINOA FLOUR AND ALMOND BUTTER ARE USED TO GIVE A PROTEIN BOOST TO A RICH, CHOCOLATY, NATURALLY SWEETENED SMOOTHIE.

1 Put all of the ingredients into a high-speed liquidizer and purée until very smooth. Pour into two glasses and sprinkle a few cacao nibs on top of each smoothie. Serve immediately.

TOASTED COCONUT AND QUINOA BREAKFAST PUDDING

VG

SERVES	4
PREP	10 minutes
COOK	35 minutes

YOU WILL NEED

1 tin (400 g/14 oz.) coconut milk

420 ml (14¼ fl oz.) coconut milk drink

60 ml (2 fl oz.) maple syrup

150 g (5¼ oz.) uncooked quinoa

1 teaspoon ground cinnamon

40 g (1½ oz.) toasted coconut

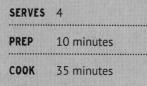

FREE FROM
DAIRY, GLUTEN & WHEAT

THIS IS CREAMY COMFORT FOOD YOU WILL WANT TO WAKE UP FOR. MILDLY SWEET, LIKE A TOASTED MARSHMALLOW, THIS PROTEIN-PACKED BREAKFAST WILL KEEP YOU GOING ALL DAY.

1 Bring the coconut milks and maple syrup to a boil in a large saucepan, whisking often, and watching carefully so the mixture does not boil over. Add the quinoa and bring it back to a boil, again taking care it does not boil over. Once it boils, reduce to the lowest heat and cover. Continue to watch the mixture for signs of over boiling for the first few minutes. Stir occasionally.

2 Cook, covered, for 25 minutes. After 25 minutes, uncover and increase the heat slightly, stir in the cinnamon and toasted coconut, and continue to cook for another 5 minutes, uncovered. Serve immediately.

THE BEST OF BOTH WORLDS: This recipe uses coconut milk from carton and tin – the carton milk cuts down on calories, while the tinned milk adds richness.

QUINOA BREAKFAST PUDDING VARIATIONS

IT'S EASY TO CUSTOMIZE YOUR BREAKFAST PUDDING BY USING CLASSIC FLAVOUR COMBINATIONS. TRY THESE ALTERNATIVE FLAVOUR VARIATIONS THAT TASTE SO GOOD THEY COULD EASILY DOUBLE AS DESSERT!

MAPLE SESAME GINGER BREAKFAST PUDDING

For a sweet-and-savoury version of this breakfast, stir in 1 tablespoon tahini and 1.25 cm (½ in.) fresh root ginger, peeled and minced, after the quinoa mixture has cooked for 25 minutes. Omit the cinnamon and coconut and continue cooking as in the main recipe on page 24.

BLUEBERRY LEMON BREAKFAST PUDDING

For a refreshing twist, try swapping the cinnamon and coconut for some fresh fruits. Stir in 75 g (2½ oz.) fresh blueberries and the juice of 1 lemon after the quinoa mixture has cooked for 25 minutes, and continue cooking as in the main recipe on page 24. Serve with a few more fresh berries on top.

WARM CARDAMOM ROSE PUDDING

For a fragrant breakfast that could double as dessert, stir in 2 drops rosewater, 2 teaspoons cardamom and 1 teaspoon saffron in place of the cinnamon and coconut, and continue cooking as in the main recipe on page 24. This pudding would also be a great end to a Moroccan or Lebanese meal.

TAHINI

Tahini is a nutrient-dense superfood with a long list of benefits. In addition to being a great source of calcium, good fats and many minerals, tahini is a complete protein, packing in more than most nuts. Make use of tahini's versatility in sweet and savoury dishes: whisk with lemon juice and maple syrup for an easy salad dressing, spread on toast or stir into your morning porridge.

PECAN QUINOA PORRIDGE

SERVES	4
PREP	5 minutes
COOK	30 minutes

YOU WILL NEED

450 ml (15 fl oz.) skimmed milk, plus extra for serving

¼ teaspoon sea salt

180 g (6¼ oz.) uncooked quinoa

2 tablespoons maple syrup, plus extra for serving

½ teaspoon ground cinnamon

75 g (2½ oz.) chopped pecan nuts

FREE FROM
GLUTEN & WHEAT

THIS IS A FABULOUS GLUTEN-FREE PORRIDGE WITH MAPLE SYRUP AND PECANS. THE QUINOA AND SKIMMED MILK MAKE IT A HEARTY YET HEALTHY BREAKFAST OPTION.

1 Bring the milk to a boil in a large saucepan, then reduce the heat and add the salt. Add the quinoa, mix well, and bring back to a boil before covering and simmering gently for 15–20 minutes.

2 Remove the lid, add the maple syrup and cinnamon, and continue to cook over a low heat for another 10 minutes, or until the quinoa porridge is thick and creamy with very little liquid left.

3 Remove from the heat, add the pecans, and serve immediately with extra maple syrup and milk.

QUINOA PORRIDGE VARIATIONS

ADD SOME MORE IDEAS TO THE QUINOA PORRIDGE POT WITH THESE VARIATIONS. QUINOA PORRIDGE MAKES THE PERFECT HEALTHY SNACK OUTSIDE OF BREAKFAST TIME, TOO.

DAIRY-FREE QUINOA PORRIDGE WITH HONEY AND TOASTED ALMONDS

Use almond milk in place of cow's milk, and replace the maple syrup with 2 tablespoons organic honey. Lightly toast 75 g (2½ oz.) flaked almonds in a non-stick frying pan until just golden brown, and sprinkle over the porridge for serving. Serve with extra almond milk and honey. Soya or oat milk can also be used in place of the almond milk.

SUMMER FRUIT AND BERRY QUINOA PORRIDGE WITH BROWN SUGAR AND VANILLA

Make the porridge as in the main recipe on page 28, but omit the cinnamon and add 2 teaspoons vanilla extract instead. Omit the maple syrup too, and add 2 tablespoons light soft brown sugar, such as demerara. Cook the porridge for a further 10 minutes after adding the vanilla and brown sugar, stirring constantly so the sugar dissolves. Serve immediately with 250 g (9 oz.) mixed summer fruit and berries such as strawberries, raspberries, blueberries, cherries and chopped peaches divided between the four bowls. Offer a bowl of brown sugar for people to add themselves.

OAT AND QUINOA PORRIDGE WITH PECANS AND DRIED APRICOTS

Cook 100 g (3½ oz.) quinoa and 75 g (2½ oz.) oats together as in the main recipe, with 450 ml (15 fl oz.) oat milk in place of skimmed milk. When the porridge is thick and creamy, add 80 g (3 oz.) chopped dried apricots along with the maple syrup, cinnamon and pecans, and mix well. Serve immediately with extra oat milk.

NUTS

Nuts not only taste delicious, but they are also an essential ingredient in lots of baking recipes, as well as being fabulous when added to salads and savoury dishes. High in dietary fibre and minerals such as potassium and magnesium, they are also rich in bone-building calcium and protein. Scatter them over desserts, pancakes, porridge and salads for an extra-healthy boost, or add them to sweet bakes, tarts and cakes for an afternoon tea treat. They are also delicious when roasted in honey and served as a snack with cocktails.

VANILLA CARDAMOM QUINOA GRANOLA

(V)

MAKES	500 g (17½ oz)
PREP	10 minutes
COOK	40 minutes, plus cooling

YOU WILL NEED

200 g (7 oz.) gluten-free rolled oats

200 g (7 oz.) uncooked quinoa

125 g (4½ oz.) shelled unsalted pistachios

60 ml (2 fl oz.) rapeseed oil

120 ml (4 fl oz.) mild honey

2 tablespoons vanilla extract

1½ teaspoons ground cinnamon

¾ teaspoon ground cardamom

¼ teaspoon fine sea salt

115 g (4 oz.) sliced almonds

FREE FROM
DAIRY, GLUTEN & WHEAT

THIS GRANOLA IS SATISFYING AND LIGHTLY SWEET. THE OATS, QUINOA AND WHOLE AND SLICED NUTS GIVE IT A GREAT TEXTURE WITH A FEW DIFFERENT TYPES OF CRUNCH. TO MAKE IT GLUTEN-FREE, BE SURE TO USE CERTIFIED GLUTEN-FREE OATS.

1 Preheat the oven to 170°C/325°F/Gas Mark 3. Line a baking tray with baking paper.

2 In a large mixing bowl, toss together the oats, quinoa and pistachios. Pour in the rapeseed oil and honey and mix well to coat evenly.

3 Sprinkle the vanilla, cinnamon, cardamom and salt over the mixture, then stir well to distribute.

4 Pour the granola onto the baking tray and spread in an even layer. Bake for 20 minutes. Briefly remove from the oven and gently, but thoroughly, stir in the sliced almonds, then spread again in an even layer. Return to the oven and continue baking until golden brown, about 20 minutes more. The granola should be gently crisp, but will crisp up more while cooling. Leave to cool on the sheet, then break apart and store in an airtight container at room temperature for up to 3 weeks.

SLIPPERY SUCCESS: Measure the oil first, then measure the honey in the same measuring cup. The honey will slide right out.

QUINOA GRANOLA VARIATIONS

WITH A FEW TWEAKS, THIS GRANOLA RECIPE CAN TAKE ON A VARIETY OF DIFFERENT FLAVOURS AND PERSONALITIES. HERE ARE SOME FAVOURITES.

(VG) (DF) (GF) (WF)

STRAWBERRY APRICOT

Immediately after baking, toss in 100 g (3½ oz.) diced dried strawberries and 120 g (4¼ oz.) chopped dried apricots. The flavours will meld while the granola cools.

(V) (GF) (WF)

DARK CHOCOLATE CHERRY

Immediately after baking, toss in 100 g (3½ oz.) dried cherries. Once the granola has cooled, add in 115 g (4 oz.) chopped dark chocolate or mini dark chocolate chips.

(V) (DF) (GF) (WF)

SPICED APPLE

Replace the pistachios and almonds with 240 g (8½ oz.) chopped walnuts or pecans. Replace the cardamom with ¼ teaspoon ground nutmeg, ¼ teaspoon ground allspice and ¼ teaspoon ground cloves. Immediately after baking, stir in 100 g (3½ oz.) chopped dried apples.

CARDAMOM

Cardamom can be an under-appreciated spice. At once warming and bracing, it's an easy way to impart a special fragrance to sweet and savoury foods alike. This recipe uses pre-ground cardamom, which is much less strong than if you grind your own. If you choose to grind your own cardamom, start with green pods rather than black. Peel off the pods and grind only the seeds in a mortar and pestle. You'll only need seeds from about 3 pods to equal the flavour of ¾ teaspoon of pre-ground spice.

QUINOA PANCAKES WITH SPICED STRAWBERRY COMPOTE AND YOGHURT

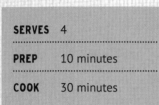

SERVES	4
PREP	10 minutes
COOK	30 minutes

YOU WILL NEED

2 eggs

240 ml (8 fl oz.) well-shaken buttermilk

180 ml (6 fl oz.) whole milk

180 g (6¼ oz.) cooked quinoa

240 g (8½ oz.) wholemeal flour

¼ teaspoon fine sea salt

1 teaspoon baking powder

½ teaspoon bicarbonate of soda

3 tablespoons maple syrup

2 tablespoons butter, melted

spray oil, for greasing

175 g (6 oz.) plain Greek-style yoghurt, for serving

FOR THE COMPOTE

560 g (20 oz.) hulled fresh strawberries

60 ml (2 fl oz.) maple syrup

1 teaspoon minced fresh root ginger

½ teaspoon ground cinnamon

⅛ teaspoon ground cardamom

2 teaspoons vanilla extract

FLUFFY WHOLEMEAL BUTTERMILK PANCAKES HARDLY NEED IMPROVEMENT, BUT THE ADDITION OF QUINOA AND A LIGHTLY SPICED COMPOTE MAKES THEM EXTRA SPECIAL.

1 First make the compote. Put the strawberries, maple syrup, ginger, cinnamon and cardamom into a small saucepan over a medium–high heat. Bring to a boil, stirring frequently. Reduce the heat to maintain a brisk simmer and add the vanilla. Cook until the strawberries are very soft and their liquid has thickened somewhat, around 10 minutes. (The liquid will continue to thicken as it cools.) Remove from the heat and smash some of the strawberries with the back of a spoon. Set to one side to cool slightly.

2 In a medium bowl, beat the eggs with a fork. Beat in the buttermilk and milk. Add the quinoa, flour, salt, baking powder, bicarbonate of soda, maple syrup and melted butter. Stir the mixture gently with a fork until there are no noticeable pockets of flour left. The batter will still be slightly lumpy.

3 Coat a non-stick frying pan with a thin layer of the spray oil and heat over a medium–high heat for a few minutes. Drop around 60 ml (2 fl oz.) batter onto the heated pan, without crowding. The batter should sizzle slightly at first. Cook until the underside is nicely browned and the top has lots of bubbles, 2–3 minutes. Then flip and cook until the other side is browned, 1–2 minutes more. Adjust the heat to cook through without burning, and add additional oil to the frying pan as necessary.

4 Serve immediately, topped with spiced strawberry compote and a dollop of yoghurt.

DAIRY-FREE BRUNCH

For a dairy-free version, use your favourite non-dairy milk and substitute a neutral tasting oil for the butter.

To make non-dairy 'buttermilk', combine 240 ml (8 fl oz.) non-dairy milk with 1 tablespoon lemon juice or apple cider vinegar. Stir and leave to sit for 10 minutes before using.

QUINOA CRÊPES WITH BERRIES AND RICOTTA (V)

SERVES	4
PREP	15 minutes, plus resting
COOK	40–50 minutes

YOU WILL NEED

125 g (4½ oz.) quinoa flour

240 ml (8 fl oz.) unsweetened rice milk

1 egg, beaten

300 g (10½ oz.) mixed berries (fresh or frozen)

2 tablespoons honey

2 tablespoons water

150 g (5¼ oz.) ricotta

2 tablespoons icing sugar

coconut oil, for frying

strips of lemon zest, for garnish

pinch of salt

(pictured on page 21)

FREE FROM GLUTEN & WHEAT

MAKING GLUTEN-FREE CRÊPES FOR BREAKFAST (AND DESSERT) IS EASY WITH QUINOA FLOUR. TOPPED WITH SWEET BERRIES AND SOFT CHEESE, THEY'RE AN INDULGENT TREAT.

1 Sift the quinoa flour and salt into a bowl. Whisk the rice milk and egg together, then slowly whisk this into the quinoa flour until you have a smooth, lump-free batter. Cover with a cloth or cling film and leave to rest for 30 minutes (or overnight in the fridge).

2 Add the berries to a saucepan with the honey and water. Gently heat for 5 minutes, stirring every so often, until the berries have just started to break down and are warmed through. Cover and put to one side.

3 Beat the ricotta in a bowl with the icing sugar. Put to one side. Heat the oven to its lowest setting.

4 Warm 1 tablespoon of coconut oil in a large frying pan. Swirl the oil around the pan to coat the bottom, and pour out any excess. Add a small ladleful of the batter to the pan. Turn and swirl the frying pan so you have a thin pancake that coats the bottom. Fry over a medium–high heat for 1–2 minutes until the crêpe is set and golden brown underneath.

5 Loosen the edge of the crêpe with a palette knife or spatula, then flip it over. Fry for another 1–2 minutes until the crêpe has coloured underneath. Slide it onto an ovenproof plate and keep warm in the oven whilst you make the other crêpes.

6 Repeat with the rest of the batter, adding more coconut oil as you need it. You should be able to make 8–12 crêpes, depending on how large you make them.

7 Serve the warm quinoa crêpes folded or rolled around the honeyed berries and whipped ricotta, garnished with lemon zest.

QUINOA CRÊPE VARIATIONS

THERE IS MORE THAN ONE WAY TO FILL A CRÊPE. HERE ARE THE FLAVOURS FROM TWO CLASSIC DESSERTS TURNED INTO CRÊPE TREATS – PLUS A WAY TO MAKE THESE CRÊPES VEGAN.

CHOCOLATE AND CACAO NIB QUINOA CRÊPES

Make the crêpes as in the main recipe, using almond milk instead of rice milk in the batter, and adding 1 teaspoon mixed spice or a pinch of cinnamon, ground ginger and nutmeg to the flour. Fry long slices of banana in coconut oil for 1–2 minutes each side so they just caramelize. Keep them warm in the oven, then fry the crêpes. Serve the crêpes and bananas with some crunchy cacao nibs and spoonfuls of yoghurt.

APPLE PIE CRÊPES

Make the crêpes as in the main recipe, using almond milk instead of rice milk in the batter. Make the filling by cooking 6 peeled, cored and chopped eating apples with ½ teaspoon ground cinnamon, ¼ teaspoon nutmeg, a pinch of ground cloves, 2 tablespoons maple syrup and 1 tablespoon water over a low heat for 5 minutes, until the apples are a little soft but not pulpy. Toast 60 g (2¼ oz.) walnut pieces in a dry frying pan for 2–3 minutes until browned. Serve the apple compote with the crêpes, walnuts, yoghurt and extra maple syrup.

VEGAN QUINOA CRÊPES

Swap the egg for 2 tablespoons melted coconut oil and make the crêpes as per the main recipe. You can use rice, coconut or soya milk in the batter. Serve the crêpes with mixed berries and coconut or soya yoghurt.

QUINOA WAFFLES WITH BERRY COMPOTE

(V)

SERVES	4
PREP	10 minutes
COOK	25 minutes

YOU WILL NEED

spray oil, for greasing

120 g (4¼ oz.) gluten-free flour

50 g (2 oz.) gluten-free rolled oats

65 g (2¼ oz.) quinoa flour

180 ml (6 fl oz.) orange juice

180 ml (6 fl oz.) non-dairy milk

3 tablespoons olive oil

1½ tablespoons sugar

2 teaspoons baking powder

1 teaspoon vanilla extract

1 teaspoon orange zest

pinch of salt

FOR THE BERRY COMPOTE

175 g (6 oz.) diced fresh strawberries

140 g (5 oz.) fresh blackberries

2 tablespoons water

2 tablespoons sugar

1 tablespoon lemon juice

pinch of salt

fresh berries, for serving

FREE FROM
DAIRY, GLUTEN & WHEAT

FINDING A GOOD GLUTEN-FREE WAFFLE RECIPE IS CHALLENGING, BUT THIS ONE HAS ADDED PROTEIN FROM QUINOA FLOUR AND STILL RETAINS A SLIGHTLY CRUNCHY OUTSIDE WITH A FLUFFY, MOIST INTERIOR.

1 Heat a shallow waffle iron (not Belgian), and make sure that it is hot by adding a couple of drops of water; they must sizzle as they hit the irons. Apply a heavy coat of spray oil to the irons.

2 Place all of the waffle ingredients in a liquidizer and purée until smooth; set aside for 10 minutes to let the batter thicken.

3 Pour the waffle batter over the iron until mostly covered, close the lid and cook for 8–10 minutes. Once the iron stops steaming, carefully lift the lid and pull out the waffle. It should be golden brown. Repeat until all of the batter has been used up.

4 While the waffles are cooking, place all of the berry compote ingredients in a small saucepan and bring to a boil over a medium heat. Adjust the stove temperature to medium–low and simmer for 15 minutes or until the liquid has turned into a syrup.

5 Divide the waffles between four plates and top with the berry compote. Serve hot.

MAKE AHEAD
You can store these
waffles, with baking
paper between them,
in the freezer for 6
months. Reheat them
in the toaster just as
you would shop-
bought waffles.

QUINOA WAFFLE VARIATIONS

AN EASY WAY TO CHANGE YOUR FAVOURITE RECIPES IS TO USE ONLY SEASONAL PRODUCE. STONE FRUITS ARE ALSO AN OPTION IN WARMER MONTHS, WHILE RICHER FLAVOURS ARE BETTER SUITED WHEN FRUITS ARE NOT IN ABUNDANCE.

PEACHES AND NECTARINES

Whenever they are in season, chop up some fresh peaches and nectarines, in equal parts, and use in place of the berries in the compote.

CHOCOLATE

These waffles would also be great with chocolate. Follow the main recipe on page 40 but replace 25 g (¾ oz.) rolled oats with the same amount of cocoa powder and top with chocolate syrup instead of compote for a decadent brunch recipe.

MAPLE CREAM

Maybe you'd like a richer topping than compote? Try whipping 240 g (8½ oz.) cream cheese or cashew cream with 3 tablespoons maple syrup and a pinch of ground cinnamon for a slightly sweet maple cream.

BERRIES

Berries are high in phytonutrients that keep your heart healthy and have anti-cancer properties. In one recent study, blackberries were shown to have the highest antioxidant value of any food tested, meaning that they are a powerful free-radical fighter and may have a positive impact on health and lower the risk of certain diseases. Strawberries also pack a surprising nutritional punch. They contain more vitamin C than oranges – roughly 160 per cent of your recommended daily allowance in just 125 g (4½ oz).

QUINOA, FETA CHEESE AND SPINACH BREAKFAST MUFFINS

MAKES	12
PREP	5 minutes
COOK	35 minutes

YOU WILL NEED

spray oil, for greasing

100 g (3½ oz.) uncooked quinoa

240 ml (8 fl oz.) water

375 g (13¼ oz.) self-raising flour

200 g (7 oz.) spinach leaves, washed, trimmed and shredded

200 g (7 oz.) crumbled feta cheese

1 tablespoon finely chopped fresh dill

300 ml (10 fl oz.) skimmed milk

100 g (3½ oz.) butter, melted

1 egg, beaten

salt and black pepper

THESE DELICIOUS AND HEALTHY LITTLE BREAKFAST MUFFINS ARE THE PERFECT WAY TO START THE DAY — AND THEY WILL KEEP YOU GOING UNTIL LUNCHTIME.

1 Preheat the oven to 200°C/400°F/Gas Mark 6. Coat a standard 12-cup muffin tin with the spray oil.

2 Put the quinoa in a saucepan with the water. Cover. Bring to a boil, then reduce the heat and gently simmer for 10–15 minutes, or until all the water has been absorbed and the quinoa is tender. If it looks like it's getting too dry while it cooks, add a splash more water. Drain well and transfer to a bowl to cool.

3 Pour the flour into a large bowl and add the spinach, crumbled feta cheese, cooked quinoa and dill. Season with salt and black pepper to taste. Stir well to combine.

4 Whisk the milk with the melted butter and beaten egg and pour into the dry ingredients. Mix with a large spoon until just combined – do not overmix as this will result in a tough texture.

5 Spoon the muffin mixture into the muffin tin and bake for 20 minutes until well risen and golden brown.

6 Carefully turn the muffins out onto a wire rack to cool; they are best served warm.

ZIP THEM UP: If you bake more muffins than you need, these can be frozen in a zip-lock bag for up to 3 months.

BREAKFAST MUFFIN VARIATIONS

TRY ONE OF THESE THREE EXTRA IDEAS ON HOW TO COOK AND SERVE THESE TASTY MUFFINS — FROM A MEAT LOVER'S VERSION TO THE PERFECT OFFICE-READY PACKED LUNCH, THERE IS SOMETHING FOR EVERYONE.

HAM AND CHEDDAR MUFFINS

Follow the main recipe on page 44. In place of the spinach and feta cheese, add 100 g (3½ oz.) chopped cooked ham and 200 g (7 oz.) grated cheddar cheese. If you would like a vegetable element, add 50 g (2 oz.) sun-dried tomatoes in olive oil, drained and finely chopped. Serve with a crunchy side salad or coleslaw.

HERBY CREAM CHEESE AND SPRING ONION MUFFIN SANDWICHES

To make the sandwich spread, mix 120 g (4¼ oz.) herb and garlic cream cheese with a small bunch of trimmed and chopped spring onions. Season to taste with salt and black pepper, then simply cut the muffins in half and spread with the cream cheese sandwich spread. Serve with salad.

TOMATO, EGG AND BACON MUFFINS

Breakfast in a muffin! Simply fry (or grill) half a tomato per person in a little olive oil until charred and soft, then place the tomato halves on the bottom half of a cut muffin; fry (or grill) 2 strips of smoked streaky bacon per person and then fry 1 egg per person, in a little olive oil or the bacon fat. Arrange the fried egg and bacon strips on top of the tomato, and place the other half of the cut muffin on top to make a sandwich. Serve with assorted sauces and relishes.

EGGS

Eggs are essential in any cook's kitchen and are a complete protein ingredient; they boast a host of vitamins such as B1, B2, B3, B5, B6, B12 and choline. Rich in folic acid too, they are nature's perfect packet of goodness. Scramble them, poach them, fry them or coddle them – they are one of the handiest ingredients for an easy, protein-rich breakfast, as well as being a requirement in most cake recipes due to their emulsifying properties.

QUINOA, CHEDDAR AND CHIVE MINI FRITTATAS (V)

MAKES	12
PREP	10 minutes
COOK	25 minutes

YOU WILL NEED

spray oil or butter, for greasing

270 g (9½ oz.) cooked quinoa

6 tablespoons finely chopped fresh chives

12 eggs

½ teaspoon fine sea salt

115 g (4 oz.) extra-sharp cheddar, grated

black pepper

FREE FROM
GLUTEN & WHEAT

MAKING FRITTATAS IN A MUFFIN TIN SETS YOU UP WITH A WEEK'S WORTH OF PORTABLE AND NUTRITIOUS BREAKFASTS AND LUNCHES. QUINOA ADDS HEFT AND FIBRE, SO YOU'LL STAY SATISFIED WHILE USING FEWER EGGS.

1 Preheat the oven to 180°C/350°F/Gas Mark 4 with a shelf in the centre. Generously spray or butter a standard 12-cup muffin tin.

2 Place 2 tablespoons of quinoa into each muffin cup. Divide the chives equally among the cups.

3 Crack the eggs into a medium bowl, add the salt and a few good grinds of black pepper, and beat with a fork until well combined. Divide the eggs equally among the muffin cups.

4 Divide the cheese among the muffin cups. Use a teaspoon to pop any bubbles and to gently distribute the cheese and chives into each frittata mix.

5 Bake for about 20–25 minutes, until the eggs are just set all the way through. (Test with a knife or cake tester.)

6 Leave to rest for 5 minutes, then gently loosen the frittatas with a rubber spatula. Serve warm from the oven or remove to a wire rack to cool completely.

FOR LUNCH: Try serving these frittatas with a side salad for a light meal.

MINI FRITTATA VARIATIONS

SINCE QUINOA AND EGGS BOTH PAIR WELL WITH MANY FLAVOURS, THE SKY'S THE LIMIT ON INTRODUCING NEW INGREDIENTS INTO THESE FRITTATAS. JUST KEEP THE TOTAL VOLUME CONSISTENT SO THEY FIT IN THE MUFFIN TINS.

V · GF · WF

ROASTED RED PEPPER AND GOAT'S CHEESE

Mince 1 roasted red pepper and add to the muffin cups on top of the quinoa, following the main recipe on page 48. Replace the cheddar with crumbled fresh goat's cheese.

V · GF · WF

SHALLOT AND GRUYÈRE

Sauté 2 shallots in 1 tablespoon olive oil, and add to the frittatas in place of the chives in the main recipe. Swap grated Gruyère for the cheddar.

V · GF · WF

SUN-DRIED TOMATO AND MOZZARELLA

Soak 3 sun-dried tomatoes in hot water for 10 minutes to soften. Mince and sprinkle over the quinoa. Replace the chives with strips of fresh basil. Replace the cheddar with diced fresh mozzarella and 25 g (¾ oz.) vegetarian Parmesan cheese, the Parmesan can be added to the eggs before beating.

QUINOA CHICKPEA SCRAMBLE BURRITO

SERVES	4
PREP	10 minutes
COOK	55 minutes

YOU WILL NEED

420 ml (14¼ fl oz.) vegetable stock

150 g (5¼ oz.) uncooked red quinoa

2 tablespoons coconut oil

225 g (8 oz.) potatoes, peeled and diced

160 g (5½ oz.) diced onion

1 tin (400 g/14 oz.) chickpeas, drained and rinsed

3 tablespoons nutritional yeast

¼ teaspoon Indian black salt/Kala Namak (optional)

180 g (6¼ oz.) fresh diced tomatoes

90 g (3¼ oz.) baby spinach

4 large wholemeal tortillas

salt and black pepper

lime wedges and salsa, for serving

(pictured on page 52)

FREE FROM
DAIRY

CHICKPEAS AND QUINOA ARE SUPER NUTRITIOUS AND TASTY WHEN COMBINED WITH POTATOES AND SPINACH. WRAPPING THEM UP INTO A BURRITO CREATES A GREAT ON-THE-GO MEAL.

1 Put the vegetable stock and red quinoa in a large saucepan, cover with a lid and bring to a boil over a medium heat. Reduce to a medium–low heat and simmer for 20–25 minutes, or until all the liquid is gone and the quinoa is tender.

2 While the quinoa is cooking, warm the coconut oil in a large frying pan over a medium heat. Once hot, add the potatoes to the pan and cook for 15 minutes, stirring occasionally so that the potatoes don't stick to the pan or burn.

3 Reduce the heat to medium–low and add the onion, sautéing for 10 more minutes, or until the potatoes are cooked through.

4 Next, mash the chickpeas in a bowl with the nutritional yeast and Indian black salt, if using, and then add to the potatoes. Cook for 5 minutes, then stir in the tomatoes and spinach, and continue heating until the spinach becomes slightly wilted.

5 Season the mixture with salt and black pepper. Carefully fold the cooked quinoa into the potato mixture, then evenly distribute the filling between the four tortillas. Fold one side and what will be the bottom of the tortilla in towards each other, and then roll tightly to make the burrito. Serve with lime wedges and your favourite salsa.

EASY DOES IT
Warm the tortillas in the oven or microwave slightly before folding them, so they are more pliable and less likely to tear.

QUINOA SCRAMBLE VARIATIONS

WHILE NEARLY EVERYONE CAN GET ON BOARD WITH BREAKFAST BURRITOS, IT'S ALWAYS A GOOD IDEA TO HAVE SOME ALTERNATIVES ON HAND AND OFFER SOME VARIETY FOR THOSE WHO ARE A LITTLE HARDER TO PLEASE.

TOFU QUINOA SCRAMBLE

If you don't like chickpeas try replacing them with 350 g (12¼ oz.) extra-firm tofu (cut into cubes), which is a lean protein; or 3 scrambled eggs for a vegetarian version. Omit the nutritional yeast and Indian black salt.

GLUTEN-FREE BREAKFAST BOWL

For a gluten-free version, make this recipe into a deliciously satisfying breakfast bowl by eliminating the tortillas, or using large lettuce leaves in place of the tortillas.

MEXICAN BEAN AND CHILLI BURRITOS

Give these burritos some Mexican flair by using the same amount of salsa instead of tomatoes, black beans instead of chickpeas, and adding some chilli powder and cumin to the filling.

SNACKS & APPETIZERS

QUINOA-DUSTED TORTILLA CHIPS WITH ARTICHOKE AND ROCKET DIP

SMOKY AUBERGINE AND QUINOA DIP

PUMPED-UP FIVE-LAYER QUINOA DIP

CHEESY HOT SAUCE QUINOA BITES

PUFFED QUINOA BHELPURI

SWEET POTATO QUINOA KIBBEH

QUINOA LETTUCE WRAPS

QUINOA-COATED FISH FINGER SANDWICH

GRILLED VEGGIE AND QUINOA SUMMER ROLLS
WITH CAJUN TAHINI SAUCE

QUINOA CRAB CAKES

Recipe on page 66

QUINOA-DUSTED TORTILLA CHIPS WITH ARTICHOKE AND ROCKET DIP

(VG)

SERVES	4
PREP	20 minutes
COOK	30 minutes

YOU WILL NEED

3 tablespoons quinoa flour

1 teaspoon onion powder

8 corn tortillas

1 tablespoon olive oil

¼ teaspoon fine salt

FOR THE DIP

175 g (6 oz.) cooked white beans, rinsed

120 ml (4 fl oz.) water

2 tablespoons olive oil

3 tablespoons quinoa flour

1½ tablespoons nutritional yeast, plus extra for topping

2 teaspoons lemon juice

½ teaspoon sea salt

pinch of freshly ground black pepper

1 tin (400 g/14 oz.) artichoke hearts in brine, drained

100 g (3 ½ oz.) baby rocket

chopped fresh coriander, for garnish

FREE FROM
DAIRY, GLUTEN & WHEAT

QUINOA FLOUR ADDS A SUBTLE NUTTY FLAVOUR TO BAKED CORN TORTILLA CHIPS, AND HELPS TO THICKEN THE DIP TOO. SERVE BOTH OF THESE WARM AND YOU HAVE AN IMMEDIATE CROWD-PLEASER AT ANY GET-TOGETHER.

1 Preheat the oven to 190°C/375°F/Gas Mark 5 and get a large baking tray out, or two smaller baking trays.

2 Stir the quinoa flour and onion powder together in a shallow bowl. Brush each tortilla with a light coating of olive oil on each side, then lay it on top of the quinoa flour and press down gently, applying a thin coating of flour on each side.

3 When all the tortillas are lightly coated with quinoa flour, lay them out on the baking tray(s) in a single layer and sprinkle with salt (you'll probably need to work in batches). Bake for 10–12 minutes, or until the tortillas are golden; some will have bubbled slightly. Take them out of the oven and set on a rack to cool. Leave the oven on, as you will need it to bake the dip.

4 Place all of the dip ingredients, except for the artichokes and rocket, in a food processor and purée until completely smooth. Add the artichokes to the food processor and pulse until the pieces are small, then transfer to a small ovenproof casserole dish. Fold in the rocket, top with ½ teaspoon of nutritional yeast and bake for 15 minutes. Wait 5 minutes for the dip to cool slightly before garnishing with coriander and serving with the chips.

SMOKY AUBERGINE AND QUINOA DIP

(VG)

SERVES	4
PREP	10 minutes
COOK	1 hour

YOU WILL NEED

250 g (9 oz.) uncooked red
quinoa

2 large aubergines

4 tablespoons extra-virgin
olive oil

4 garlic cloves, peeled

80 g (3 oz.) black olives,
pitted and roughly
chopped

80 g (3 oz.) sun-dried
tomatoes in oil, drained
and roughly chopped

2 tablespoons fresh
marjoram, finely chopped

zest and juice of 1 lemon

1 tablespoon balsamic
vinegar

salt and black pepper

fresh crusty bread or
vegetable crudités,
for serving

FREE FROM
DAIRY, GLUTEN
& WHEAT

THIS SMOKY DIP MADE WITH RED QUINOA, AUBERGINE, SUN-DRIED TOMATOES AND PLUMP OLIVES MAKES A WONDERFUL VEGETARIAN SANDWICH FILLING AS WELL AS THE PERFECT SAUCE FOR PASTA OR ROASTED VEGETABLES.

1 Preheat the oven to 220°C/425°F/Gas Mark 7.

2 Put the quinoa in a saucepan with 300 ml (10 fl oz.) cold water. Cover. Bring to a boil, then reduce the heat and gently simmer for 10–15 minutes, or until all the water has been absorbed and the quinoa is tender. If it looks like it's getting too dry while it cooks, add a splash more water. Drain well and transfer to a bowl.

3 Meanwhile, cut the aubergines in half lengthwise and score the flesh on the inside. Put them in a roasting tin and drizzle with 3 tablespoons of olive oil. Bake for 45–50 minutes until the flesh is soft, adding the garlic cloves for the last 10 minutes. Leave to cool.

4 Scoop out the flesh of the aubergines and add to a bowl with the garlic, cooked quinoa and the rest of the ingredients. Mix well.

5 Adjust the seasoning to taste with the salt and pepper, and serve warm or at room temperature with crusty bread, or try fresh crudités for a gluten-free option.

PUMPED-UP FIVE-LAYER QUINOA DIP

(VG)

SERVES	4
PREP	17 minutes
COOK	20 minutes

YOU WILL NEED

200 g (7 oz.) uncooked quinoa

360 ml (12 fl oz.) tomato juice

1 tin (400 g/14 oz.) refried beans

20 g (¾ oz.) nutritional yeast

1 fresh jalapeño, seeded and chopped

½ head iceberg lettuce, chopped

2 tomatoes, diced

1 avocado, pitted and cubed

tortilla chips, for serving

FREE FROM
DAIRY, GLUTEN & WHEAT

THIS BRIGHTLY COLOURED CROWD-PLEASING PARTY FAVOURITE IS A PROTEIN-PACKED UPDATE ON AN OLD CLASSIC, AND WILL BE WELCOME AT ANY GATHERING!

1 In a medium pan over a high heat, bring the quinoa and tomato juice to a rolling boil. Reduce the heat to a simmer, cover, and cook for 20 minutes. Remove from the heat and fluff with a fork.

2 In a medium bowl, combine the refried beans with the nutritional yeast and chopped jalapeño.

3 You can make individual servings as shown, or for a bigger gathering, use a large shallow bowl or baking dish (20 × 20 cm/ 8 × 8 in.), and spread the refried bean-jalapeño mixture evenly to create a base layer. Spoon the tomato quinoa over the beans evenly, as the second layer. The third layer is the chopped lettuce, followed by the diced tomatoes and avocado cubes. Serve with tortilla chips.

PARTY PERFECT: Use small glasses or plastic cups to make individual servings – great for a stand-up party.

CHEESY HOT SAUCE QUINOA BITES

(VG)

MAKES	20
PREP	15 minutes, plus freezing
COOK	25 minutes

YOU WILL NEED

80 g (3 oz.) non-dairy mozzarella

1 tin (400 g/14 oz.) cannellini beans, drained and rinsed

270 g (9½ oz.) cooked quinoa (cooked in vegetable stock)

1 garlic clove, minced

120 ml (4 fl oz.) gluten-free hot sauce or buffalo wing sauce

½ teaspoon celery salt

½ teaspoon paprika

salt and black pepper

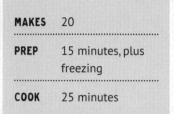

FREE FROM DAIRY, GLUTEN & WHEAT

THESE FLUFFY, SPICY BITES CAN BE SERVED AS FINGER FOOD WITH DRINKS, OR AS APPETIZERS. EITHER WAY, THEY ARE FLAVOURFUL AND DIPPABLE. SERVE WITH A COOL RANCH DIP TO BALANCE THE SPICY COATING.

1 Cut the mozzarella into small 1.25 cm (½ in.) cubes and freeze for at least 1 hour, or longer if possible, so that the pieces take on a firmer consistency.

2 Preheat the oven to 180°C/350°F/Gas Mark 4. Line a baking tray with baking paper.

3 In a food processor, process the beans to a crumbly paste, about 30 seconds. Scrape down the sides using a spatula, add 90 g (3¼ oz) cooked quinoa, and then process for another 30 seconds.

4 Transfer the mixture to a mixing bowl, and combine with the remaining 180 g (6¼ oz.) quinoa, the garlic, ½ teaspoon each of salt and black pepper, 60 ml (2 fl oz.) of hot sauce, the celery salt and paprika.

5 With your hands, scoop out a 2.5 cm (1 in.) piece of dough, and mould it into a rustic ball shape around a frozen cube of cheese. Place on a baking tray.

6 Continue to make the balls, spacing them 2.5 cm (1 in.) apart on the baking tray, until all of the quinoa mixture and cheese are used.

7 Bake the bites for 15 minutes, then brush with the remaining hot sauce and bake for another 10 minutes.

8 Let the bites sit for several minutes to cool before serving, otherwise the cheese will be very hot and runny and the bites will fall apart.

QUINOA BITES VARIATIONS

CHEESY BITES ARE THE IDEAL WAY TO CRAM YOUR FAVOURITE FLAVOURS INTO A PROTEIN-PACKED, HAND-HELD PARTY SNACK. TRY PIZZA, JALAPEÑO PEPPER OR BROCCOLI-CHEDDAR FLAVOURS FOR JUST AS MUCH TASTE AND FUN.

VG **DF** **GF** **WF**

CHEESY PIZZA BITES

To the bean-quinoa mixture in the main recipe, add 60 ml (2 fl oz.) tomato purée and I small bunch chopped fresh basil in place of the hot sauce, celery salt and paprika.

VG **DF** **GF** **WF**

JALAPEÑO PEPPER BITES

To the bean-quinoa mixture in the main recipe, add 2 fresh jalapeño peppers, finely diced, in place of the hot sauce, celery salt and paprika.

V **DF** **GF** **WF**

BROCCOLI-CHEDDAR BITES

To the bean-quinoa mixture in the main recipe, add 135 g (4¾ oz.) broccoli florets, finely chopped, in place of the hot sauce, celery salt and paprika. Wrap around frozen cubes of cheddar instead of mozzarella.

BROCCOLI

Broccoli is a superfood powerhouse, rich in many vitamins and minerals, and a flavonoid that makes broccoli an anti-inflammatory wonder as well. Many like broccoli florets best as a raw dippable snack, while others enjoy them lightly steamed. Roasting or blackening brings a great flavour, and combining broccoli with cheese is a winning combination!

PUFFED QUINOA BHELPURI

(VG)

MAKES	8
PREP	30 minutes
COOK	5 minutes

YOU WILL NEED

50 g (2 oz.) puffed quinoa

1 red onion, peeled and diced

2 tomatoes, cored and diced

4 ready-made poppadums, broken up into small pieces

50 g (2 oz.) chopped dried dates

handful of fresh coriander, stalks and leaves chopped

handful of fresh mint, leaves chopped

100 g (3½ oz.) pomegranate seeds

2 teaspoons cumin seeds

juice of 1 lime

1 tablespoon tamarind paste

1 teaspoon demerara sugar

salt

FREE FROM
DAIRY, GLUTEN & WHEAT

BHELPURI IS A SAVORY INDIAN SNACK MADE FROM PUFFED RICE AND SERVED IN PAPER CONES. THIS VERSION USING QUINOA IS JUST AS DELICIOUS AND MAKES A GREAT NIBBLE WITH DRINKS.

1 Warm a dry frying pan over a medium heat and pour in the puffed quinoa. Stir and cook for 1–2 minutes until the quinoa turns golden and smells nutty. Transfer to a large bowl.

2 Stir the red onion, tomatoes, poppadums, dates, coriander, mint and pomegranate seeds into the quinoa.

3 Put the cumin seeds into the frying pan. Stir and cook over a medium heat for 1–2 minutes until the seeds smell nutty and begin popping. Add them to the poppadum mixture.

4 Whisk the lime juice with the tamarind paste, sugar and a pinch of salt. Taste and add more salt and sugar if you think it needs it. Stir into the bhelpuri and serve immediately.

PUFF IT UP:

Puffed (or popped) quinoa is made by heating grains of quinoa until they pop. They are great as a cereal or for adding crunch to salads and dishes like this bhelpuri.

To make puffed quinoa, heat a saucepan over a medium heat and add a handful of the grains so that they coat the base in one layer. Cover the saucepan and heat the quinoa, shaking it every so often as you would for popcorn, until you can hear it beginning to pop. Keep shaking the saucepan and once the popping starts to slow down, take it off the heat and transfer the quinoa to a bowl. Let it cool, then store in an airtight container and use within a couple of days.

For a crisper result, warm 1 tablespoon sunflower or vegetable oil in the saucepan before adding the quinoa.

KEEP IT FRESH
The dressing is a tangy combination of tamarind, lime juice and a pinch of sugar. Add it just before serving so the poppadums and quinoa stay crunchy.

SWEET POTATO QUINOA KIBBEH

(VG)

SERVES	4–8
PREP	20 minutes
COOK	1 hour

YOU WILL NEED

3 sweet potatoes, peeled and chopped into small chunks

100 g (3½ oz.) uncooked quinoa

big handful of fresh coriander, stalks and leaves chopped

1 teaspoon allspice

1 teaspoon ground cumin

1 teaspoon ground coriander

pinch of cayenne pepper

1 small onion, finely chopped

40 g (1½ oz.) pine nuts, toasted

extra-virgin olive oil

salt and black pepper

salad leaves, for serving

FREE FROM
DAIRY, GLUTEN
& WHEAT

IN THE LEVANT, KIBBEH IS A DEEP-FRIED SNACK MADE WITH LAMB. THIS VERSION IS A HEALTHY VEGAN TAKE USING NUTS AND GRAINS, ALL BOUND TOGETHER WITH SWEET POTATO.

1 Preheat the oven to 180°C/350°F/Gas Mark 4.

2 Bring a large saucepan of water to a boil and add the chopped sweet potatoes. Cover and simmer for 10 minutes, until the potatoes are just starting to soften.

3 Add the quinoa to the sweet potatoes. Simmer for another 10–15 minutes until both are tender and the sweet potatoes are soft when you press them with a fork. Drain well.

4 Put the sweet potatoes and quinoa back into the saucepan. Mash over a low heat until the sweet potatoes are smooth and any excess water has evaporated.

5 Add the fresh coriander, allspice, cumin, ground coriander, cayenne pepper, onion and pine nuts to the saucepan with a good pinch of salt and black pepper. Stir the mixture together. Taste and add more seasoning if you think it needs it.

6 Grease a 1 litre (35 fl oz.) ovenproof dish with a splash of olive oil. Spoon the kibbeh into the dish and smooth over the top. Bake for 30 minutes, or until the top is golden brown.

7 Mark the kibbeh into slices as soon as it comes out of the oven – four, six or eight slices, depending on how many people you want to serve.

8 Leave the kibbeh in its dish for 10–15 minutes to cool a little before serving with salad.

QUINOA LETTUCE WRAPS

(VG)

MAKES	10
PREP	10 minutes
COOK	30 minutes

YOU WILL NEED

360 ml (12 fl oz.) vegetable stock

100 g (3½ oz.) uncooked tricolour quinoa

½ tablespoon chilli powder

2 teaspoons ground cumin

½ teaspoon smoked paprika

½ teaspoon ground coriander

½ teaspoon salt

⅛ teaspoon cayenne pepper

2 teaspoons avocado oil

75 g (2½ oz.) diced red onion

75 g (2½ oz.) diced yellow or orange pepper

175 g (6 oz.) cooked black beans or kidney beans, rinsed and drained

90 g (3¼ oz.) roasted sweetcorn (thawed if frozen)

15 g (½ oz.) fresh coriander, finely chopped

1 tablespoon lime juice

10 round lettuce leaves

salt and black pepper

lime wedges, for garnish

FREE FROM
DAIRY, GLUTEN & WHEAT

THESE LEAVES ARE GREAT FOR SERVING AT PARTIES BECAUSE OF THEIR SIZE, AND YOU DON'T NEED UTENSILS TO EAT THEM.

1 Put the vegetable stock, quinoa, chilli powder, cumin, paprika, coriander, ½ teaspoon of sea salt and cayenne pepper in a saucepan, cover, and bring to a boil over a medium heat. Reduce to a medium–low heat and simmer for 20 minutes, or until all of the liquid is gone and the quinoa is tender.

2 In a large frying pan, warm the avocado oil over a medium heat. Once hot, add the red onion to the pan and sauté for 3 minutes or until mostly translucent. Next, add the pepper, black beans and sweetcorn. Cook for an additional 2 minutes, stirring occasionally.

3 Adjust the heat to medium–low and add the cooked quinoa to the frying pan. Season with salt and black pepper, then incorporate the coriander and lime juice into the mixture.

4 Divide the filling between the lettuce leaves, garnish each lettuce wrap with a lime wedge, and serve immediately.

SERVING STYLE: Different kinds of lettuce will provide different shapes, although softer lettuce is less messy to eat as you can roll it as you go. Serve each leaf in a silicone muffin case if you prefer.

QUINOA LETTUCE WRAP VARIATIONS

HAVING A RECIPE THAT IS MADE UP OF A FILLING AND SHELL MEANS THAT YOU CAN EASILY CHANGE THE VESSEL OR ADD SOME FLAIR TO THE FILLING WITHOUT TOO MUCH COMPROMISE.

ASIAN-INSPIRED

To make an Asian-inspired version of these lettuce wraps, substitute 1 teaspoon fresh root ginger for the spices, replace the black beans with edamame or grilled chicken (for a non-vegan version), use water chestnuts instead of sweetcorn, and toss the filling in 60 g (2¼ oz.) hoisin sauce and 1 teaspoon liquid aminos.

TACO SHELLS

This spicy aromatic quinoa filling would also be great in small, crunchy taco shells served as an appetizer.

NACHO PLATTER

Make an awesome nacho platter by spreading out 250 g (9 oz.) tortilla chips and topping them with the quinoa filling from the main recipe. Sprinkle cheddar cheese on top and bake for 15 minutes at 150°C/300°F/Gas Mark 2.

GINGER
Ginger has been used in Asian and Indian cuisine for centuries, and also has a long history of being used to relieve gastro-intestinal discomfort. This spicy root contains numerous anti-inflammatory and antioxidant compounds that benefit your health.

QUINOA-COATED FISH FINGER SANDWICH

SERVES	4
PREP	15 minutes
COOK	15 minutes

YOU WILL NEED

150 g (5¼ oz.) quinoa flakes

1 tablespoon fresh flat-leaf parsley, finely chopped

zest of 1 lemon

400 g (14 oz.) firm white fish such as cod, haddock, hake, pollock or coley

plain flour, for coating

1 egg, beaten

4 granary bread rolls, cut in half

salt and black pepper

lemon wedges, lettuce, sliced tomatoes and light mayonnaise, for serving

FREE FROM
DAIRY

MAKE YOUR OWN DELICIOUS FISH FINGERS FOR THE ULTIMATE SANDWICH. QUINOA IS USED AS A CRUNCHY COATING WHICH TASTES GREAT WITH LETTUCE LEAVES AND A TOASTED BUN.

1 Preheat the oven to 200°C/400°F/Gas Mark 6, and line a large baking tray with baking paper.

2 Mix the quinoa flakes with the parsley and lemon zest, and season to taste with salt and black pepper.

3 Cut the fish fillets into thin strips. Dip them in the flour then the egg and then coat them in the quinoa flake mixture. Chill for 10–15 minutes.

4 To cook the fish fingers, arrange them in one layer on the lined baking tray and bake for 15 minutes until they are golden brown, turning them halfway through cooking.

5 For serving, place some lettuce and a sliced tomato on the bottom half of each bread roll, divide the fish fingers between the rolls, and then add a dollop of mayonnaise on top of the fish. Place the second half of the bread roll on top to make a sandwich. Serve with extra salad and fries to make a hearty meal.

GRILLED VEGGIE AND QUINOA SUMMER ROLLS WITH CAJUN TAHINI SAUCE

(VG)

SERVES	4
PREP	15 minutes
COOK	30 minutes

YOU WILL NEED

240 ml (8 fl oz.) vegetable stock

60 g (2¼ oz.) uncooked quinoa

olive oil, for grilling

115 g (4 oz.) portobello mushrooms, cut into 8 slices

1 medium courgette cut into 16 thin strips

1 large carrot, cut into 16 thin strips

16 mangetout, stems trimmed

8 sheets round rice paper

1 medium avocado, cut into 8 thin slices

FOR THE CAJUN TAHINI SAUCE

60 ml (2 fl oz.) tahini

3 tablespoons water

1 tablespoon rice wine vinegar

1 tablespoon lime juice

1 teaspoon sriracha hot sauce

¼ teaspoon liquid smoke

pinch of salt

FREE FROM DAIRY, GLUTEN & WHEAT

THIS RECIPE REVAMPS A STANDARD SUMMER ROLL BY INCORPORATING GRILLED VEGETABLES, SEASONED QUINOA AND A SMOKY DIPPING SAUCE. THE FLAVOURS SCREAM SUMMER BUT GIVE YOU A REASON TO EAT HEALTHY ANY TIME OF THE YEAR.

1 Put the vegetable stock and quinoa in a saucepan, cover, and bring to a boil over a medium heat. Reduce to a medium–low heat and simmer for 20–25 minutes, or until all the liquid is gone and the quinoa is tender. Transfer the quinoa to a bowl and set aside to cool.

2 Bring a grill or griddle pan up to a medium heat, lightly coat with the olive oil, and spread the mushroom slices, courgette, carrot and mangetout over it. Grill for 3 minutes or until the vegetables are slightly charred, then flip over and grill for another 3 minutes. Set the grilled vegetables aside to cool slightly.

3 Place warm water in a wide, shallow dish and gently submerge a sheet of rice paper in it for 4–5 seconds, lift it out, and drip dry.

4 Lay the rice paper flat and spoon 1½–2 tablespoons of quinoa just off-centre in a rectangular shape. Place 1 slice of mushroom, 2 sticks of courgette, 2 sticks of carrot, 2 mangetout pods and 1 slice of avocado on top of the quinoa, working quickly.

5 Fold two sides of the rice paper in, width-wise, and roll the remainder up tightly, without tearing it. Repeat steps 3–5 for the remaining rolls.

6 For the sauce, whisk together all of the ingredients in a small bowl until smooth, and serve with the rolls.

QUINOA CRAB CAKES

SERVES	4
PREP	55 minutes
COOK	50 minutes

YOU WILL NEED

spray oil, for greasing

100 g (3½ oz.) uncooked quinoa

240 ml (8 fl oz.) fish or vegetable stock

180 g (6¼ oz.) cooked crabmeat (tinned or fresh)

1 small red chilli, finely diced

2 spring onions, finely chopped

½ teaspoon garlic granules

½ teaspoon smoked paprika

zest of 1 lemon

cornflour, to coat

salt and black pepper

lemon or lime wedges, yoghurt or soured cream dressing, and salad or fresh coriander leaves, for serving

FREE FROM
DAIRY, GLUTEN & WHEAT

SPICY LITTLE QUINOA CRAB CAKES ARE EASY TO MAKE AND ARE PERFECT AS AN APPETIZER OR LIGHT LUNCH. SERVE THESE CRAB CAKES WITH A HOMEMADE TOMATO SAUCE AND SALAD LEAVES OR A LIGHT YOGHURT OR SOURED CREAM DRESSING.

1 Preheat the oven to 200°C/400°F/Gas Mark 6. Coat a large baking tray with spray oil.

2 Cook the quinoa in the stock for 15–20 minutes, or until all the liquid has been absorbed and the quinoa is fluffy. Remove from the heat and leave to cool for 10 minutes.

3 In a mixing bowl combine the quinoa with all of the other ingredients, except the cornflour, and mix well. Cover the mixture and let it firm up in the fridge for 30–45 minutes.

4 Form the mixture into 12 little patties, dip them in the cornflour to coat, and place the crab cakes on the baking tray. Bake for 30 minutes, or until they are crisp and golden brown. You may need to turn them over halfway through cooking so that they colour evenly.

5 Serve immediately with wedges of lemon or lime, yoghurt or dressing, a sprinkle of coriander, and salad.

FISH CAKES
Fish can be used in place of the crab — use any firm white fish such as cod, haddock, pollock or monkfish.

MAIN COURSES

QUINOA PIZZA WITH BLUE CHEESE AND AUBERGINE

SPROUTED QUINOA CHIRASHI SUSHI BOWL

SPROUTED QUINOA AND SALMON TEMAKI SUSHI

QUINOA BEAN BURGER WITH BASIL AÏOLI

SPICY PEANUT VEGGIE STEW WITH QUINOA DUMPLINGS

VEGETABLE PAELLA-STYLE QUINOA

CHIPOTLE SWEET POTATO QUINOA ENCHILADAS

BLACK BEAN, QUINOA AND VEGETABLE CHILLI

RISOTTO-STYLE QUINOA WITH CARAMELIZED ONIONS AND MUSHROOMS

SMOKY SPANISH QUINOA WITH CHICKEN AND CHORIZO

LAMB AND QUINOA MEATBALLS

Recipe on page 102

QUINOA PIZZA WITH BLUE CHEESE AND AUBERGINE

SERVES	2
PREP	20 minutes
COOK	45 minutes

YOU WILL NEED

1 aubergine, cut into thin strips

extra-virgin olive oil, for frying

½ tin (200 g/7 oz.) chopped tomatoes

1 teaspoon dried oregano

75 g (2½ oz.) crumbled blue cheese

salad, for serving

FOR THE BASE

150 g (5¼ oz.) uncooked quinoa, soaked for 8 hours or overnight, and drained

60 ml (2 fl oz.) water

1 egg

1 teaspoon baking powder

½ teaspoon sea salt

2 tablespoons olive oil

FREE FROM
GLUTEN & WHEAT

THIS DELICIOUS GLUTEN-FREE PIZZA IS HEALTHY AND LOADED WITH TRUSTY CHEESE, VEGETABLES AND HERBS. ONCE THE BASE IS MADE YOU CAN ADD ANY TOPPINGS YOU LIKE.

1 Preheat the oven to 220°C/425°F/Gas Mark 7 and line a 23 cm (9 in.) tart or cake tin with baking paper.

2 Put all of the pizza base ingredients in a liquidizer and blend on high until the mixture resembles a thick pancake batter.

3 Pour the base batter into the prepared tin and bake for 30 minutes until it is crisp and set firm. Ease the base out of the pan and put it on a lined pizza tray.

4 While the base is cooking, fry the aubergine strips in a little olive oil until soft and just charred on the edges.

5 To assemble the pizza, spoon the tomatoes over the base, sprinkle with oregano and then arrange the cooked aubergine strips over the top. Sprinkle on the blue cheese and bake for 10–15 minutes, until the cheese has melted and the topping is hot.

6 Serve immediately with salad.

TIME SAVING TIP: The base batter can be frozen, so make extra and freeze the mixture you don't use for fast future meals.

QUINOA PIZZA VARIATIONS
THERE'S NO NEED TO SERVE TAKEAWAY — THIS BASIC QUINOA PIZZA DOUGH IS A CROWD-PLEASING AND INVALUABLE RECIPE FOR YOUR GLUTEN-FREE KITCHEN.

(GF) (WF)

HAWAIIAN CHEESY QUINOA PIZZA

Add 100 g (3½ oz.) grated cheddar cheese to the base and bake as in the main recipe on page 82. When the base is cooked, add the toppings in the following order: ½ tin (200 g/7 oz.) chopped tomatoes; ½ teaspoon dried oregano; 100 g (3½ oz.) chopped cooked ham; 4 tinned pineapple rings, drained and diced; 75 g (2½ oz.) grated mozzarella cheese. Bake in a preheated oven at 220°C/425°F/Gas Mark 7 for 10 minutes, or until the cheese has melted and is bubbling. Serve the pizza with salad.

(V) (GF) (WF)

INDIVIDUAL MARGHERITA QUINOA PIZZAS

Make the quinoa base batter as described on page 82, but pour the batter into 2 × 4-hole Yorkshire pudding tins, or into an 8-hole shallow tart tin. Bake for 20 minutes until the bases have set and are crisp. Leave to cool for 5 minutes and then ease them out of the tins gently and place them on a greased baking tray. Add the toppings in the following order: ½ tin (200 g/7 oz.) chopped tomatoes mixed with 1½ teaspoons dried oregano, 1 tablespoon tomato purée and 1 teaspoon sugar, then 150 g (5¼ oz.) mozzarella cheese, torn into small pieces. Bake the individual pizzas for about 5 minutes, until the sauce is hot and the cheese has melted. Serve warm or cold with salad and olives.

(GF) (WF)

SPICY MEAT FEAST QUINOA PARTY PIZZA

This meaty and spicy version of the pizza is rectangular and can be served cut into small squares, which makes it perfect finger food. Make the base as described on page 82, but spoon it into a well-greased and lined rectangular dish or tray, about 22 x 12 cm (9 x 5 in.). Bake until crispy. Add the toppings in the following order: ½ tin (200 g/7 oz.) chopped tomatoes, mixed with 1 teaspoon of dried chilli powder, 1 tablespoon tomato purée and 1 teaspoon of sugar; 50 g (2 oz.) sliced peppered salami; 50 g (2 oz.) diced cooked ham; 50 g (2 oz.) diced Spanish chorizo; 1 teaspoon capers, drained; and 100 g (3½ oz.) grated smoked cheddar cheese. Bake for 10–15 minutes, until the topping is cooked and the cheese has melted. Let the pizza cool for 5 minutes before cutting into squares and serving.

TOMATOES

Tomatoes, whether fresh or tinned, count towards your five-a-day and are packed with vitamins, including C, B6 and E. They also contain folic acid, which is essential for bone development and cell regrowth. Tomatoes can be eaten raw or cooked, and are the basis of many popular family recipes. Unless you need a smooth purée or sauce, there is no need to discard the skin or the seeds.

SPROUTED QUINOA CHIRASHI SUSHI BOWL

MAKES	1
PREP	15 minutes, plus sprouting
COOK	5 minutes

YOU WILL NEED

200 g (7 oz.) sprouted quinoa

2 tablespoons rice wine vinegar

2 tablespoons sesame seeds

1 egg

½ tablespoon sugar

1 teaspoon mirin

rapeseed or sunflower oil for the frying pan or omelette pan

75 g (2 ½ oz.) mangetout

3.5 cm (1 ½ in.) chunk of cucumber, sliced

100 g (3 ½ oz.) fresh sushi-grade tuna, sliced

100 g (3 ½ oz.) fresh sushi-grade salmon, sliced

small handful of cress

pickled ginger and tamari or gluten-free soya sauce, for serving

FREE FROM
DAIRY, GLUTEN & WHEAT

CHIRASHI SUSHI MEANS 'SCATTERED SUSHI' AND IT'S THE PERFECT TREAT FOR FANS OF THE DELICATE ART OF SUSHI MAKING. SPROUTED QUINOA MAKES A LIGHT ALTERNATIVE TO SUSHI RICE.

1 Put the sprouted quinoa in a bowl. Add the rice wine vinegar and sesame seeds, and stir together. Spoon the quinoa mixture into your serving bowl.

2 Beat the egg with the sugar and mirin. Warm a little oil in a small frying pan or omelette pan over a low heat. Pour in the omelette mixture. Swirl the frying pan so the bottom is evenly coated, and let the egg cook until it's almost set in the middle. Loosen the edges with a spatula, flip the omelette over, and cook for 10–20 seconds. Slide it out of the frying pan. Let the omelette cool for a few minutes, then roll it up and slice it.

3 While the omelette is cooking, fill a saucepan with water and bring it to a boil. Add the mangetout. Simmer without a lid for 2 minutes, so that they are just blanched. Drain and rinse them under cold water.

4 Top the quinoa with the sliced omelette, mangetout, cucumber, tuna and salmon. Serve topped with cress, with pickled ginger and tamari or soya sauce on the side.

ABOUT SPROUTS: For tips on sprouting quinoa, turn to page 91.

CHIRASHI BOWL VARIATIONS

ONCE YOU'VE GOT YOUR BOWL OF SEASONED SPROUTED QUINOA, YOU CAN MIX AND MATCH YOUR FAVOURITE TRADITIONAL — AND NOT-SO-TRADITIONAL — SUSHI TOPPINGS. TRY THE RECIPES BELOW FOR A BIT OF VARIATION, OR WHY NOT INVENT YOUR OWN COMBINATIONS?

RAW VEGAN CHIRASHI BOWL

Following the main recipe on page 86, season the sprouted quinoa with the vinegar and sesame seeds then top it with a mixture of sliced avocado, carrot, cucumber, red pepper, red onion, sweetcorn and shredded nori. Dress the sushi bowl with a squeeze of lemon juice and serve with some pickled ginger, soya sauce and wasabi.

SMOKED SALMON AND PICKLED CUCUMBER CHIRASHI BOWL

Slice half a cucumber as thinly as possible. Put it in a bowl with 60 ml (2 fl oz.) rice wine vinegar, 2 tablespoons sugar and ½ tablespoon coarse or flaked salt. Leave it for 30 minutes while you make the sweet omelette per the main recipe. Stir 2 tablespoons of the cucumber brine into the sprouted quinoa with the sesame seeds. Top the quinoa with the pickled cucumber, 115 g (4 oz.) smoked salmon, a couple of cooked prawns, sliced omelette and some shiso, sorrel or baby spinach.

TOFU, GREEN BEAN AND TOMATO CHIRASHI

Pat a 200 g (7 oz.) block of tofu dry with kitchen towel and slice it into small chunks. Sprinkle the tofu with a little salt and 1 tablespoon cornflour. Turn it over a few times to coat it in the cornflour. Warm a splash of sunflower or rapeseed oil in a frying pan. Add the tofu and fry for 2 minutes until the tofu doesn't stick to the pan. Flip it over and fry until it's golden on both sides. Put it in a bowl. Mix together 1 tablespoon mirin and 1 tablespoon light soya sauce and pour it over the tofu. Simmer 200 g (7 oz.) green beans for 2–3 minutes until just tender. Drain. Divide the sprouted quinoa between two serving bowls, then top with the tofu, green beans, 6 halved baby plum tomatoes per person and a couple of shredded spring onions. Drizzle the sauce from the tofu over the chirashi for serving.

SPROUTED QUINOA AND SALMON TEMAKI SUSHI

MAKES	2
PREP	10 minutes, plus sprouting
COOK	2 minutes

YOU WILL NEED

100 g (3 ½ oz.) sprouted quinoa

1 tablespoon rice wine vinegar

1 tablespoon sesame seeds

1 sheet of nori

2 sticks cucumber

1 tablespoon shredded daikon

60 g (2¼ oz.) sushi grade salmon, sliced into sticks

salt and black pepper

pickled ginger and tamari or gluten-free soya sauce, for serving

(pictured on page 90)

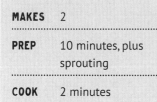

FREE FROM
DAIRY, GLUTEN & WHEAT

TEMAKI HAND ROLLS ARE THE EASIEST KIND OF SUSHI TO MAKE. YOU JUST NEED SHEETS OF NORI, SOME SPROUTED QUINOA AND A FEW STRIPS OF FISH, VEG OR OMELETTE. NO NEED FOR YEARS OF STUDY, NO SPECIAL TOOLS, YOU CAN JUST GET ROLLING.

1 Place the sprouted quinoa in a bowl. Stir in the rice wine vinegar with a pinch of salt until thoroughly combined.

2 Pour the sesame seeds into a dry frying pan. Toast over a low heat for 1–2 minutes, until the sesame seeds are golden. Keep stirring while they toast so they don't burn. Stir them into the quinoa.

3 Slice the sheet of nori in half so you have two rectangles. Make sure your hands are dry, and take the end of one sheet in your left hand if you're right-handed, the right if you're left-handed. Heap half of the quinoa onto the nori and flatten it with the back of a spoon.

4 Top the quinoa with 1 stick of cucumber and half the shredded daikon, placed on the quinoa at a diagonal, pointing toward the empty end of the nori. Lay a few strips of salmon on top.

5 Roll the nori around the sprouted quinoa tightly on the diagonal to make a cone-shaped roll.

6 Repeat with the other sheet of nori and fillings to make 2 rolls. Serve with pickled ginger and tamari or soya sauce.

TEMAKI ROLL VARIATIONS

YOU CAN PUT ALMOST ANYTHING IN A TEMAKI HAND ROLL — THINK OF IT LIKE A SANDWICH AND MIX AND MATCH FILLINGS UNTIL YOU GET THE PERFECT TEMAKI BLEND.

NEED SOME INSPIRATION? TRY SOME OF THESE COMBINATIONS

- Strips of smoked salmon and sliced avocado
- Flaked smoked mackerel and sliced cooked beetroot
- Shredded cooked chicken and sliced mango
- Strips of sweet omelette (see page 86), shredded spring onions and slices of red pepper
- Strips of grilled pepper, rare steak and rocket
- Blanched asparagus spears and smoked trout
- Strips of raw tuna, shredded spring onions and wasabi mayonnaise
- Sliced, grilled Portobello mushrooms, cooked beetroot and spinach
- Fried tofu steaks, cucumber and sliced radishes
- Diced prawns combined with mayo, sriracha and shredded spring onions.

Why not try your favourite sashimi flavours in a temaki roll?

HOW TO SPROUT QUINOA

Sprouting is the traditional practice of germinating seeds, nuts, grains and legumes under controlled conditions to increase their nutritional content and make them more easily digestible.

Sprouted quinoa is easy to make and is a delicious addition to salads, sandwiches and other dishes. Sprouting jars are commonly available or you can get them via the internet — or you can make your own. To make about 200 g (7 oz.) of sprouted quinoa:

- Rinse 200 g (7 oz.) of quinoa under running water until the water turns clear.

- Place the rinsed quinoa in a 2 litre (70 fl oz.) sprouting jar and fill it with cold filtered water. Leave for about 6 hours.

- Drain the water and put on the sprouting lid. (A sprouting lid is a piece of fine mesh that replaces the sealed lid insert.) Place the jar upside down in a bowl to catch drips.

- A few times a day, rinse the sprouts with plenty of clean water and place the jar back in the bowl to drain. In a day or two, you should see lots of little sprouts.

- Spread the sprouts on a clean plate and cover with kitchen towel. Let the sprouts dry out. Then store in an airtight container in the fridge for up to 2 weeks.

QUINOA BEAN BURGER WITH BASIL AÏOLI

(VG)

SERVES	6
PREP	20 minutes
COOK	40 minutes

YOU WILL NEED

1 tablespoon freshly ground flaxseed

1 tin (400 g/14 oz.) cannellini beans, drained, rinsed and mashed

180 g (6¼ oz.) cooked quinoa

125 g (4½ oz.) potatoes, roasted and mashed

15 g (½ oz.) nutritional yeast

½ red onion, finely diced

large handful of fresh basil, very finely diced

2 garlic cloves, minced

2 tablespoons gluten-free plain flour, plus extra for forming the burgers

80 ml (3 fl oz.) vegan mayonnaise

2 tablespoons basil pesto

salt and black pepper

gluten-free buns and lettuce, for serving

FREE FROM
DAIRY, GLUTEN & WHEAT

THIS SAVOURY BURGER IS PACKED WITH FRESH HERBS AND IS THE PERFECT TREAT AT THE END OF A LONG DAY.

1 Preheat the oven to 180°C/350°F/Gas Mark 4.

2 Combine the flaxseed with 3 tablespoons of warm water. Set aside to gel. (This process is often called making a flax 'egg'.)

3 Combine the beans, quinoa, potatoes, nutritional yeast, onion, basil and garlic in a large bowl, and stir or use your hands to incorporate the ingredients. Add the flour and the flaxseed gel, and combine completely. Using flour (flour your hands and have a plate of flour to work with), form burgers 9 cm (3½ in.) round and 1.5 cm (½ in.) thick (or slightly smaller if you prefer).

4 Transfer the burgers to a baking tray and bake for 40 minutes, flipping them after 20 minutes.

5 To make the basil aïoli, put the vegan mayonnaise in a bowl with the basil pesto and stir until combined.

6 Serve the burgers with fresh buns, lettuce and a bowl of the aïoli on the side.

A LIGHTER OPTION: Instead of a bun, try serving the burgers wrapped in lettuce leaves for a low-carb option.

QUINOA BURGER VARIATIONS

MIX UP YOUR BEAN BURGERS BY STACKING THEM WITH COLOURFUL VEGGIES, TRYING DIFFERENT BEANS AND ROOTS, OR PAIRING COOL, TANGY LEMON AÏOLI WITH HEARTY LENTILS. THE BEST WAY TO FINISH THE BLACK-BEAN BUTTERNUT BURGER IS ON THE BARBECUE — CRISPY GOODNESS GALORE!

BLACK-BEAN BUTTERNUT BURGER

Omit the basil, swap the cannellini beans for black beans, and replace the mashed potatoes with roasted, mashed butternut squash per the recipe on page 92. This burger tastes great with chipotle aïoli. To make it, combine 80 ml (3 fl oz.) vegan mayonnaise with 1 tinned chipotle pepper in adobo, very finely chopped.

RAINBOW STACK BURGERS

Omit the basil in the main recipe. Garnish the burger with slices of tomato, orange pepper, avocado and red onion. Spread the bun with yellow mustard and a tangy sauce made by combining 80 ml (3 fl oz.) vegan mayonnaise with 3 tablespoons of tomato ketchup.

HEARTY LEMON LENTIL BURGERS

Omit the basil in the main recipe. Reduce the quantity of cooked quinoa to 135 g (4¾ oz.). Replace the cannellini beans with 250 g (9 oz.) cooked lentils and the juice and zest of 1 lemon, reserving 1 tablespoon of the juice. To make the lemon aïoli, combine 80 ml (3 fl oz.) vegan mayonnaise with the tablespoon of lemon juice.

BUTTERNUT SQUASH

The butternut is a favourite among the succulent squash fruits, and the status is well earned. Butternut squash is rich in antioxidants, vitamins, phytonutrients and minerals. It contains a significant amount of fibre and is naturally low in fat. Brightly coloured and vibrantly flavoured, butternut squash is incredibly versatile, which makes it great for savoury and sweet options. Try it in sweet bread recipes, warming soups, layered into a lovely lasagna or tucked into a veggie burger.

SPICY PEANUT VEGGIE STEW WITH QUINOA DUMPLINGS

(VG)

SERVES	6–8
PREP	20 minutes
COOK	50 minutes

YOU WILL NEED

2 tablespoons olive oil

1 onion, chopped

1–2 garlic cloves, minced

3 large carrots, scrubbed and diced

3 stalks celery, diced

2 tins (800 g/28 oz.) chopped tomatoes

20 g (¾ oz.) sliced cremini mushrooms

1 red pepper, seeded and diced

1 jalapeño, seeded and diced

2 l (70 fl oz.) vegetable stock

160 g (5½ oz.) peanut butter

2 teaspoons chilli flakes (adjust according to heat preference)

salt and black pepper

FREE FROM
DAIRY, GLUTEN & WHEAT

THIS HEARTY, FLAVOUR-PACKED STEW INCLUDES FLUFFY QUINOA DUMPLINGS AND IS A COMFORT ON COLDER NIGHTS.

1 Heat the olive oil in a saucepan over a medium heat, and sauté the onion, garlic, carrots and celery until the onion is translucent. Add the tomatoes, mushrooms, pepper, jalapeño, stock, peanut butter and chilli flakes to taste, and let the stew mixture simmer for 20–30 minutes, stirring occasionally, until the vegetables have softened but have some bite. Add salt and black pepper to taste.

2 To make the dumplings, sift together the flours, baking powder, onion powder and salt. Add the soda water and olive oil, stirring twice around the bowl. Add the quinoa and stir until just combined; do not overstir – the batter can be just slightly 'together'.

3 Increase the heat to high and bring the stew to a boil. Drop the dumpling dough in small spoonfuls into the stew and cook for 10 minutes. Cover and steam for another 8–10 minutes until the dumplings are tender. Once the dumplings are fully cooked and the stew is removed from the heat, do not cover the pot, as the dumplings will continue to steam and will overcook.

FOR THE DUMPLINGS

120 g (4 oz.) rice flour
90 g (3 oz.) plain flour
1 tablespoon baking powder
1 tablespoon onion powder
1 teaspoon salt
180 ml (6 fl oz.) soda water
1½ tablespoons olive oil
90 g (3 oz.) cooked quinoa

VEGETABLE PAELLA-STYLE QUINOA

(VG)

SERVES	4
PREP	20 minutes
COOK	35 minutes, plus resting

YOU WILL NEED

½ teaspoon saffron threads

60 ml (2 fl oz.) hot water

80 ml (3 fl oz.) olive oil

1 onion, finely diced

3 fresh tomatoes, seeded and chopped

4 garlic cloves

2 teaspoons smoked paprika

1 teaspoon fine sea salt (less if the stock is salty)

1 l (35 fl oz.) vegetable stock

1 dried bay leaf

300 g (10½ oz.) uncooked quinoa

150 g (5¼ oz.) frozen artichoke quarters, defrosted

150 g (5¼ oz.) peas, fresh or frozen

150 g (5¼ oz.) cut green beans, fresh or frozen

3 piquillo peppers, drained and sliced

black pepper

lemon wedges, for serving

**FREE FROM
DAIRY, GLUTEN
& WHEAT**

SPANISH PAELLA IS RENOWNED FOR THE DELICIOUS FLAVOUR COMBINATION OF SMOKY PAPRIKA WITH FRAGRANT SAFFRON. THIS VEGETARIAN VERSION RETAINS THE AROMATICS OF THE TRADITIONAL RECIPE, BUT HAS THE ADDED TEXTURE OF QUINOA.

1 Crumble the saffron threads into a small bowl and pour over the hot water. Let it sit for 10 minutes to make saffron-flavoured liquid.

2 Heat the olive oil over a medium–high heat in a cast-iron frying pan. Add the onion, tomato, garlic, paprika, ½ teaspoon of salt and cook, stirring from time to time, until the onion is softened and lightly translucent. This should take about 10 minutes.

3 Add the stock, saffron and soaking liquid, bay leaf, remaining ½ teaspoon of salt and a few grinds of black pepper; stir and bring to a boil over a high heat. Sprinkle in the quinoa and arrange evenly across the surface of the pan. Reduce the heat as necessary to simmer until most of the liquid has been absorbed, about 15 minutes. Do not stir. If the burner does not heat the pan evenly, rotate the pan every once in a while, so that the mixture is evenly heated.

4 Scatter the artichokes, peas, green beans and peppers evenly throughout the frying pan, pressing down gently to submerge some of the vegetables beneath the surface. Continue simmering, without stirring, until all of the liquid is absorbed, about 7 minutes more. Then turn up the heat all the way and cook undisturbed for 3 minutes. At this stage you should hear the paella crackling gently. Take the pan off the heat to sit for 10 minutes before serving.

STUNNING SOCARRAT
One of paella's distinguishing features is the socarrat, the crisp, dark crust that forms on the bottom of the frying pan. Using quinoa instead of rice makes a socarrat a little trickier to achieve, but it can be done. Using a cast-iron frying pan to retain extra heat, and a quick high-heat period at the end of cooking will ensure that your meal includes some delicious crispy bits.

PAELLA-STYLE QUINOA VARIATIONS

THIS DISH IS BURSTING WITH FLAVOUR IN ITS VEGAN INCARNATION, BUT IF YOU LIKE SEAFOOD, YOU CAN'T BEAT THE VERSION WITH PRAWNS AND MUSSELS. QUINOA PAIRS BEAUTIFULLY WITH THE BRINY FLAVOURS OF THE SEA.

DF GF WF

SEAFOOD PAELLA

Peel and de-vein 450 g (I lb.) extra-large prawns and season with salt. When the oil is heated, cook the prawns for about 2 minutes per side, until just barely cooked through. Transfer to a plate. Bring a small amount of water to a boil in a saucepan with a lid. Add 16 cleaned mussels and steam until they open, discarding any that don't open. To cook the quinoa, replace the vegetable stock with seafood stock and follow the main recipe. Omit the artichokes and arrange the seafood over the paella.

V DF GF WF

PUT AN EGG ON IT!

This variation might not pass a Spanish authenticity test, but smoked paprika is a natural companion to both fried eggs and paella. Fry an egg in a generous glug of olive oil until crispy around the edges, and sprinkle with a little salt and smoked paprika. To get crispy edges without overcooking, don't flip the egg. Instead, flick a few drops of water into the frying pan halfway through cooking and quickly place a lid on top. The steam will gently cook the top of the egg while the bottom crisps over the direct heat. Follow the main recipe to make the paella.

DF GF WF

PAELLA-STYLE QUINOA WITH CHICKPEAS AND CHORIZO

Spanish chorizo is a dried and cured sausage. It is flavoured with smoked paprika and goes beautifully with paella, as well as with chickpeas. You can use vegan chorizo-style sausage as an alternative. To make this variation, slice a Spanish chorizo link and brown the pieces on both sides in 2 tablespoons of the olive oil before adding the remaining oil, onion, tomato and other ingredients per the main recipe. When brown, remove to a kitchen towel-lined plate and set aside. Add I tin (400 g/I4 oz.) chickpeas and the browned sausage pieces along with the peas, green beans and peppers. Omit the artichokes.

SAFFRON

Saffron is a wonderfully aromatic spice that lends both deep flavour and vibrant colour to food. It has been revered in numerous cultures – from India to Rome – since ancient times. You'll find it in very small packages containing just a pinch of its fragile threads. Each thread is one stamen of a crocus flower (and flowers contain only 3 stamens each). The threads are carefully harvested by hand in a laborious process, which is one reason why saffron is among the most expensive spices in the world. Luckily a little goes a long way, so you can enjoy saffron in paella and other dishes without breaking the bank.

CHIPOTLE SWEET POTATO QUINOA ENCHILADAS

MAKES	4
PREP	25 minutes
COOK	1 hour 15 minutes

YOU WILL NEED

2 large sweet potatoes, cut into cubes

2 tablespoons olive oil

200 g (7 oz.) uncooked quinoa

240 ml (8 fl oz.) tomato juice (or water, or stock)

2–3 tinned chipotle peppers in adobo, chopped

4 large wholemeal tortillas

350 g (12¼ oz.) cooked sweetcorn

1 tin (400 g/14 oz.) black beans

120 g (4¼ oz.) non-dairy soured cream

3 tablespoons almond milk

salt and black pepper

3 plum tomatoes, seeded and diced, for garnish

1 avocado, peeled, pitted and diced, for garnish

handful chopped fresh coriander, for garnish

YOU CAN ADJUST THE QUANTITY OF CHIPOTLE PEPPERS IN THIS RECIPE TO SUIT YOUR TASTE FOR SPICE. TOPPING WITH COOL AVOCADO IS A NICE BALANCE.

1 Preheat the oven to 180°C/350°F/Gas Mark 4. Prepare a baking tray by lining it with baking paper.

2 Arrange the sweet potato in a single layer on the baking tray, drizzle with the olive oil, and season with salt and black pepper. Roast for 25 minutes, until the potato is tender.

3 In a medium saucepan over a high heat, bring the quinoa, tomato juice and 120 ml (4 fl oz.) water to a rolling boil. Reduce to a simmer, cover, and cook the mixture for 18–20 minutes, until all the liquid is absorbed. Stir in the chipotle peppers.

4 In a dry frying pan over a low heat (or for a few seconds in the microwave), warm the tortillas individually before filling. Spoon 3–4 tablespoons of cooked quinoa down the middle of each tortilla. Top with a quarter of the sweetcorn, black beans and roasted potato. Roll and place open-side down in a 20 × 20 cm (8 x 8 in.) baking dish. Repeat with the remaining tortillas until the dish is full of enchiladas.

5 Cover with aluminium foil and bake for 30 minutes. Remove the foil and continue cooking for another 5–7 minutes.

6 Thin the soured cream with the almond milk and drizzle over the enchiladas. Scatter with the diced tomatoes and avocado, and top with the fresh coriander, for serving.

BLACK BEAN, QUINOA AND VEGETABLE CHILLI (V)

SERVES	8
PREP	10 minutes
COOK	45 minutes

YOU WILL NEED

2 tablespoons olive oil

1 red onion, diced

1 green pepper, diced

4 garlic cloves, minced

2 tablespoons tomato purée

1 tablespoon chilli powder

1 teaspoon smoked paprika

1 teaspoon ground cumin

½ teaspoon dried oregano

720 ml (24 fl oz.) good vegetable stock

200 g (7 oz.) uncooked red quinoa

1 sweet potato, peeled and cut into 1.5 cm (½ in.) dice

2 tins (800 g/28 oz.) black beans, drained and rinsed

2 tins (800 g/28 oz.) chopped tomatoes

350 g (12¼ oz.) sweetcorn kernels (thawed if frozen)

salt

30 g (1 oz.) chopped fresh coriander

diced avocado, grated cheese, soured cream and lime wedges, for serving

FREE FROM GLUTEN & WHEAT

THIS RECIPE MAKES A BIG BATCH OF HEARTY, DEEPLY FLAVOURED CHILLI. IT ONLY IMPROVES THE FOLLOWING DAY, SO IT'S EQUALLY GOOD FOR MAKING IN ADVANCE OF A PARTY, FOR A COUPLE OF FAMILY DINNERS OR FOR A WEEK'S WORTH OF LUNCHES.

1 In a medium saucepan, heat the olive oil over a medium–high heat. Add the onion and pepper and a sprinkle of salt, and cook, stirring from time to time until softened, about 5 minutes. Add the garlic, tomato purée, chilli powder, smoked paprika, cumin and oregano, and cook, stirring frequently – about 2 minutes more.

2 Add the stock and the remaining salt, the quinoa and the sweet potato. Raise the heat to high, bring to a boil, then cover and reduce the heat to a simmer for 20 minutes.

3 Add the beans, tomatoes and sweetcorn and simmer for 15 minutes more. Uncover for the last 5 minutes to reduce the sauce a bit. Taste and adjust for salt. Stir in the coriander.

4 Ladle the chilli into bowls and serve with the diced avocado, cheese, soured cream and lime wedges.

RISOTTO-STYLE QUINOA WITH CARAMELIZED ONIONS AND MUSHROOMS

Ⓥ

SERVES	4
PREP	20 minutes
COOK	1 hour 30 minutes, plus resting

YOU WILL NEED

8 dried shiitake mushrooms

1 teaspoon herbes de Provence

1 dried bay leaf

1 l (35 fl oz.) vegetable stock

1 teaspoon fine sea salt, if needed

3 tablespoons butter

3 tablespoons olive oil

3 onions, peeled, halved and sliced thinly from tip to root

120 ml (4 fl oz.) dry white wine

225 g (8 oz.) shiitake mushrooms, stems removed and sliced

225 g (8 oz.) cremini mushrooms, sliced

2 teaspoons soya sauce

(continued)

THIS RECIPE PACKS THE FLAVOUR PUNCH OF A REAL ITALIAN RISOTTO DISH, SATISFYING YOUR CRAVING FOR CREAMY, COMFORTING GOODNESS.

1 Place the dried shiitakes, herbes de Provence and bay leaf in a small pan and pour in the stock. If the stock is unsalted, add ¾ teaspoon of fine sea salt. Bring the mixture to a boil, then cover and simmer for 5 minutes. Remove from the heat and let the mixture steep while you caramelize the onions. If you have the time, steep the mixture for several hours or overnight to get the best flavour.

2 In a 30 cm (12 in.) frying pan, heat 1 tablespoon of the butter and 1 tablespoon of the olive oil over a medium to medium–low heat. When melted, add the onions. Cook, undisturbed, for 10 minutes – you want to hear a gentle sizzle – then stir gently, scraping up any brown bits on the bottom of the frying pan, and add ¼ teaspoon of salt. Continue cooking on medium to medium–low heat, stirring occasionally, for 35–50 minutes more, until the onions are substantially reduced in volume, soft but not mushy, and beautifully browned. Don't be tempted to raise the heat even if it's hard to be patient – but do lower it slightly if necessary to prevent burning. Deglaze the frying pan with 1 tablespoon of the wine, then raise the heat and cook for another minute until the wine has evaporated. Place the onions in a small bowl.

(continued)

300 g (10½ oz.) uncooked quinoa

1 teaspoon finely chopped fresh thyme leaves

50 g (2 oz.) grated vegetarian Parmesan cheese, plus extra for serving

15 g (½ oz.) finely chopped fresh flat-leaf parsley

ground black pepper

3 In the same frying pan, melt 1 tablespoon of butter with 1 tablespoon of the olive oil over a medium–high heat. Add the shiitakes, creminis and soya sauce. Simmer undisturbed for 2–3 minutes, then stir frequently while cooking until the mushrooms have released and reabsorbed any juices as well as browning nicely. They should substantially decrease in volume, about 5–10 minutes. Deglaze the pan with 1 tablespoon of wine. Set the mushrooms aside in a bowl.

4 In the same frying pan, melt the remaining tablespoon of butter with the remaining tablespoon olive oil over a medium–high heat. Add the quinoa and cook, stirring constantly, until lightly fragrant, 2–3 minutes. Add the remaining wine and cook, stirring, until absorbed. Raise the heat to high, add the thyme and ladle in the stock one or two ladlesful at a time, leaving the dried mushrooms and bay leaf in the pan to discard later. Cook until the stock is nearly absorbed before adding more. Stir frequently. This process will take about 15 minutes. When the last of the broth is almost absorbed, turn off the heat and cover the pan. Let the risotto sit for 10 minutes to allow it to thicken.

5 Stir in the onions, mushrooms, Parmesan, parsley and a few good grinds of black pepper. Serve the risotto in bowls with extra fresh grated Parmesan cheese to pass around.

ADVANCE PLANNING: Caramelizing the onions is a bit time-consuming, but you can do it up to a few days in advance.

QUINOA-STYLE RISOTTO VARIATIONS

QUINOA RISOTTO IS JUST AS ADAPTABLE AS TRADITIONAL RISOTTO IN TERMS OF BOTH FLAVOUR AND FORMAT. HERE ARE SOME SUGGESTIONS TO GET YOU STARTED, BUT FEEL FREE TO MAKE CHANGES ON THIS THEME WITH WHATEVER SEASONAL INGREDIENTS YOU HAVE AVAILABLE.

QUICK RISOTTO

For a much quicker risotto with a similar flavour profile, omit the caramelized onions. Dice I onion and sauté until it is soft and translucent (this process should take about 7 minutes). Add the quinoa and proceed as directed in the main recipe.

SPRINGY RISOTTO

Omit the fresh and dried mushrooms, soya sauce and thyme per the main recipe. Add 150 g (5¼ oz.) peas; I bunch thin-stemmed asparagus, cut into 2.5 cm (I in.) lengths; and 2 tablespoons chopped fresh tarragon, 5 minutes before the end of cooking. If desired, stir in II5 g (4 oz.) crumbled fresh goat's cheese along with the Parmesan.

RISOTTO CAKES

Beat I egg in a medium bowl, add up to 360 g (12½ oz.) leftover risotto-style quinoa, and mix well. Sprinkle 60 g (2¼ oz.) panko or dry breadcrumbs onto a plate. Form the risotto mixture into small patties and dredge in the breadcrumbs to coat. Heat a thin layer of oil in a frying pan over a medium–high heat and cook the patties in batches until golden brown on each side and heated through.

SMOKY SPANISH QUINOA WITH CHICKEN AND CHORIZO

SERVES	2
PREP	15 minutes
COOK	30–35 minutes

YOU WILL NEED

pinch of saffron threads

240 ml (8 fl oz.) hot chicken stock

extra-virgin olive oil, for frying

2 skinless, boneless chicken breasts, chopped

75 g (2½ oz.) Spanish chorizo, skinned and diced

1 onion, finely chopped

1 red pepper, roughly chopped

1 green pepper, roughly chopped

1 garlic clove, minced

2 teaspoons smoked paprika

100 g (3½ oz.) uncooked quinoa

salt and black pepper

fresh flat-leaf parsley and lemon wedges, for serving

FREE FROM
DAIRY, GLUTEN & WHEAT

FLAVOURED WITH SAFFRON, GARLIC AND PAPRIKA, PAELLA IS ONE OF THOSE GREAT DISHES THAT CAN ALWAYS BE ADAPTED. QUINOA IS USED HERE INSTEAD OF RICE, WITH CHICKEN AND CHORIZO TO MAKE IT A REALLY HEARTY DISH.

1 Add a pinch of saffron threads to the hot chicken stock and let them soak for a few minutes until they start to release their colour. Give the stock a stir to thoroughly disperse the flavour.

2 Warm a splash of olive oil in a deep frying pan. Add the chicken. Fry over a medium heat for 5 minutes until the chicken is browned all over. Stir every so often so it gets an even colour. Lift out of the frying pan with a slotted spoon or spatula and put it on a plate.

3 Add the chorizo to the frying pan. Stir and fry for 2 minutes until it has browned a little and released plenty of red, spicy oils.

4 Add the onion and peppers to the pan. Season with salt and black pepper. Cook and stir for 5 minutes until the vegetables are starting to soften. Stir in the garlic and smoked paprika.

5 Add the chicken along with any juices from the plate, then stir in the quinoa. Pour in the saffron chicken stock and cover.

6 Bring the quinoa mixture to a boil, then turn the heat down. Gently simmer for 10–15 minutes, until the stock has been absorbed and the quinoa is tender.

7 Taste and adjust the seasoning according to preference. Serve scattered with sprigs of flat-leaf parsley and lemon wedges for squeezing.

SMOKY SPANISH QUINOA WITH SEAFOOD AND CHORIZO

Swap the diced chicken for 2 skinned and chopped fillets of firm white fish such as cod, haddock, whiting, hake or pollock. Don't fry it at the beginning, but add once most of the stock has been absorbed so it cooks for 5–8 minutes. You can also add a handful of cleaned mussels or clams to the frying pan with the fish, if you like. The fish should be white and opaque and the shellfish should be open when the quinoa is ready (discard any shells that don't open).

LAMB AND QUINOA MEATBALLS

SERVES	4
PREP	15 minutes, plus chilling
COOK	1 hour

THIS DISH HAS A MIDDLE EASTERN TWIST, WITH SWEET AND SHARP POMEGRANATE MOLASSES IN THE SAUCE. QUINOA IS ADDED TO THE MEATBALL MIXTURE TO KEEP IT LIGHT AND MOIST.

YOU WILL NEED

50 g (2 oz.) uncooked quinoa

120 ml (4 fl oz.) water

250 g (9 oz.) lamb mince

2 garlic cloves, minced

1 mild red chilli, minced

1 small onion, finely chopped

handful of fresh flat-leaf parsley, leaves and stalks finely chopped

1 tablespoon tahini

pinch of cayenne pepper

olive oil, for frying

salt and black pepper

FOR THE TOMATO SAUCE

1 onion, finely chopped

1 long red pepper, finely chopped

2 garlic cloves, minced

1 teaspoon sumac

1 tin (400 g/14 oz.) chopped tomatoes

1 tablespoon pomegranate molasses

salt and black pepper

cooked quinoa and fresh coriander, for serving

1 Put the quinoa in a saucepan with the water. Cover, bring to a boil, then turn the heat and gently simmer for 10–15 minutes, or until all the water has been absorbed and the quinoa is tender and fluffy. If it looks like it's getting too dry while it cooks, add a splash more water. Drain well.

2 Transfer the cooked quinoa to a bowl. Add the lamb, garlic, chilli, onion, parsley leaves and stalks, and tahini. Season with a pinch of cayenne and salt and black pepper. Knead everything together for a few minutes until well mixed.

3 Pull a lump off the meatball mixture and roll into a ball about the size of a walnut, then put it on a plate. Repeat with the rest of the mixture until you have about 24 meatballs. Cover the plate with cling film and chill in the fridge for an hour or overnight so the meatballs firm up (or 15 minutes in the freezer).

4 Warm a splash of olive oil in a deep frying pan over a medium heat. Add the meatballs. Gently fry for 5–6 minutes until the meatballs are lightly browned. Turn a few times so they brown evenly.

5 Lift the meatballs out of the frying pan with a slotted spoon or spatula, put them on a plate and set aside.

(continued)

FREE FROM
DAIRY, GLUTEN & WHEAT

6 Make the sauce. Add the onion and red pepper to a saucepan. Season with salt and black pepper. Keep the heat low and gently cook for 10 minutes until the onion and pepper are soft but not coloured – give them a stir every now and then.

7 Add the garlic and sumac to the saucepan. Cook and stir for 1–2 minutes until the saucepan smells sweet and aromatic. Stir in the chopped tomatoes and pomegranate molasses. Stir 200 ml (7 fl oz.) hot water into the sauce.

8 Add the meatballs back to the saucepan and cover. Turn up the heat so the sauce starts to simmer, then turn it down again so it's just simmering gently. Cook for around 20 minutes, until the sauce has thickened a little. Stir every now and then.

9 While the meatballs and sauce simmer, cook some more quinoa to serve with the meatballs – 200 g (7 oz.) simmered in 480 ml (16 fl oz.) water for 10–15 minutes should be enough for 4 people.

10 Taste the tomato sauce and add more salt and pepper if you think it needs it. Serve the meatballs and tomato sauce with the cooked quinoa and fresh, chopped coriander.

Sumac is a fragrant spice that is commonly used in Middle Eastern cooking. It originates from the Sumac bush and is made by drying and crushing the berries. Sumac has a lemony flavour and is commonly used as a garnish or part of the Za'atar spice mix.

QUINOA MEATBALLS VARIATION

THERE'S MORE THAN ONE WAY TO TURN A MEATBALL INTO A MEAL. FROM ROMANTIC MEATBALLS AND SPAGHETTI TO SHARE, TO A WRAP YOU CAN EAT ON THE GO, SEE WHICH STYLE SUITS YOU — OR TRY THEM ALL!

MIX UP YOUR MEATBALLS

Lamb pairs well with Middle Eastern flavours, but you can swap the lamb mince for beef, pork or turkey if you prefer. Try using different herbs and spices too, depending on what you have at home and what you like.

SIDE SWAPS

If you want to have a different side dish, try bulgur wheat. Soak 40 g (1½ oz.) per person in enough hot water to cover it, just like couscous. Leave it for 20 minutes, then drain it (if you need to) and stir in lots of freshly chopped parsley before serving it with the meatballs and tomato sauce. And, although it isn't a traditional Italian meatball and sauce mix, this recipe is also yummy with spaghetti or tagliatelle.

LAMB AND QUINOA MEATBALL WRAPS

Make the meatballs following the main recipe but instead of frying, grill them for 10–12 minutes, turning once, so they are browned and cooked through — you can thread them onto skewers to make them easier to turn. Serve them wrapped in flatbreads with chopped lettuce, cucumber, tomatoes, red onion and fresh parsley. A spoonful of dairy-free tzatziki or cashew cream and some ground cumin are also delicious with the wraps.

SOUPS, SALADS & SIDES

ROASTED CAULIFLOWER QUINOA SOUP

CURRY SQUASH QUINOA BISQUE WITH COCONUT CREAM

QUINOA COUSCOUS WITH BLOOD ORANGES AND BURRATA

QUINOA KISIR WITH POMEGRANATE AND WALNUTS

SUMMER QUINOA SALAD WITH GRAPEFRUIT TAHINI DRESSING

FRUITY QUINOA TABBOULEH WITH FETA CHEESE

BEETROOT AND CARROT QUINOA CAKES WITH CUMIN YOGHURT SAUCE

THAI-STYLE CRAB, POMELO AND QUINOA SALAD

ROASTED WINTER VEGETABLE, QUINOA AND WILD RICE SALAD

Recipe on page 118

ROASTED CAULIFLOWER QUINOA SOUP

(VG)

SERVES	4
PREP	10 minutes
COOK	40 minutes

YOU WILL NEED

450 g (1 lb.) head of cauliflower, core cut out and chopped into florets

160 g (5½ oz.) diced onion

2 teaspoons olive oil

1 tin (400 g/14 oz.) chopped tomatoes

480 ml (16 fl oz.) vegetable stock

450 g (1 lb.) cooked white quinoa

200 g (7 oz.) kale, washed, de-stemmed and chopped

1 tablespoon finely chopped fresh basil

2 tablespoons finely chopped fresh flat-leaf parsley

salt and black pepper

(pictured on page 117)

FREE FROM
DAIRY, GLUTEN & WHEAT

IF YOU'RE LOOKING FOR A PLANT-BASED SOUP THAT IS AS FILLING AS IT IS FLAVOURFUL, YOU NEED TO MAKE THIS RECIPE. ROASTED CAULIFLOWER ADDS DEPTH, THE HERBS BRING FRESHNESS AND THE QUINOA MAKES IT SUBSTANTIAL.

1 Preheat the oven to 190°C/375°F/Gas Mark 5 and line a baking tray with baking paper.

2 Toss the cauliflower florets and onion in the olive oil, ½ teaspoon of salt and ¼ teaspoon of black pepper until evenly covered. Spread the mixture out in a single layer on the baking tray and roast for 20 minutes.

3 Once the cauliflower is roasted, transfer it to a large saucepan, warmed over a medium heat. Add the tomatoes, vegetable stock, 240 ml (8 fl oz.) water, and quinoa to the pan and bring to a boil.

4 Reduce the heat to medium—low, and add the kale, basil and parsley to the pan. Stir and simmer for 15 minutes, covered.

5 Check the soup occasionally and add more water or vegetable stock if you feel that it is not thin enough. Season with salt and pepper and serve warm.

QUINOA SOUP VARIATIONS

A WARM SOUP LIKE THIS IS COMFORTING AND SATISFYING BUT THERE ARE MORE WAYS TO ADAPT IT TO FIT A DIFFERENT SEASON OR INCREASE THE HEARTINESS FOR COLD NIGHTS.

SAUSAGE OR BEANS

For an even more filling soup, add a couple of sliced links of your favourite gluten-free sausage, or a tin of cannellini beans for a low-fat option.

AUTUMNAL PUMPKIN

Give this recipe seasonal flavours by substituting pumpkin purée for the tomatoes, and using fresh thyme and sage instead of the basil and parsley.

SOURDOUGH BOWL

This cauliflower soup would be great served in a toasted sourdough bread bowl. Just scoop out a rough sourdough loaf until the walls are 2.5 cm (I in.) thick, brush the outside with a thin coat of garlic olive oil, and bake for 5 minutes at 190°C/375°F/Gas Mark 5, then fill with soup.

CURRY SQUASH QUINOA BISQUE WITH COCONUT CREAM

(VG)

SERVES	4
PREP	15 minutes
COOK	45 minutes

YOU WILL NEED

1.35 kg (3 lb.) kabocha squash, peeled and chopped

4 garlic cloves

1 tablespoon olive oil

½ teaspoon salt

720 ml (25 fl oz.) vegetable stock

reserved liquid from coconut milk

380 g (13½ oz.) cooked quinoa

2 tablespoons yellow curry powder

salt and white pepper

2 tablespoons chopped fresh chives, for serving

FOR THE COCONUT CREAM

1 tin (400 ml/14 fl oz.) full-fat coconut milk, refrigerated overnight

1 teaspoon lime juice

¼ teaspoon salt

FREE FROM
DAIRY, GLUTEN & WHEAT

WHO WOULD HAVE THOUGHT THAT QUINOA COULD LEND CREAMINESS TO BISQUE WITHOUT THE UNNECESSARY FAT FROM DOUBLE CREAM? THIS CURRIED BISQUE IS SUPER-COMFORTING AND SEEMS INDULGENT, TOO.

1 To make the coconut cream, separate the hardened coconut fat from the liquid and place it in a bowl. Keep the liquid for the bisque. Whisk the coconut fat with the lime juice and salt, and put it in the fridge until ready for serving.

2 Preheat the oven to 190°C/375°F/Gas Mark 5, and line a large baking tray with baking paper. Toss the squash and garlic with the olive oil, salt and ¼ teaspoon of white pepper in a large bowl. Spread the mixture on the baking tray and roast for 30 minutes.

3 Once the squash is roasted, put it in a liquidizer or food processor with the vegetable stock, liquid from the coconut milk, quinoa and curry powder. Purée until smooth – you may need to work in batches, depending on the size of your liquidizer.

4 Transfer the puréed bisque to a large pot and bring to a boil over a medium heat, stirring occasionally so that the bottom does not burn. Adjust the heat to low and simmer, covered, for 10 minutes, again stirring occasionally.

5 Taste and season with more salt and white pepper if necessary. Divide the soup between four bowls and top with a large dollop of coconut cream and a few sprinkled chives. Serve immediately.

SQUASH SWAP
Can't find kabocha squash? Try using the same volume of butternut or acorn squash instead.

QUINOA COUSCOUS WITH BLOOD ORANGES AND BURRATA

(V)

SERVES	4
PREP	5 minutes
COOK	15 minutes

YOU WILL NEED

2 tablespoons olive oil

200 g (7 oz.) uncooked quinoa

zest and juice of 1 lemon

30 g (1 oz.) pine nuts

2 tablespoons chopped fresh flat-leaf parsley, plus extra for garnish

1 tablespoon chopped fresh mint leaves, plus extra for garnish

2 blood oranges, peeled and cut into segments

250 g (9 oz.) burrata cheese

salt and black pepper

crusty bread, for serving

FREE FROM
GLUTEN & WHEAT

THIS ELEGANT QUINOA COUSCOUS SALAD IS SERVED WITH JUICY SLICES OF BLOOD ORANGE AND CREAMY BURRATA CHEESE. IT IS PERFECT FOR A LIGHT SUMMER LUNCH OR AN ALFRESCO SUPPER.

1 Heat the olive oil in a large saucepan that has a lid, and add the quinoa, lemon zest and juice, and pine nuts. Sauté over a low heat and stir to cover all the grains with the oil and toast the nuts, before adding 450 ml (15 fl oz.) water along with the parsley and mint.

2 Simmer, covered, with the lid on for 15 minutes, until the quinoa is cooked and has absorbed all of the liquid.

3 Season to taste with salt and black pepper and allow the dish to come to room temperature.

4 For serving, create a table centrepiece by using a single bowl, or divide the quinoa between four plates and arrange the sliced blood oranges around the edge of each. Break the burrata into 4 pieces if making individual servings or leave it whole and place it in the middle of the quinoa. Garnish with extra parsley and mint, and serve with crusty bread.

COUSCOUS SALAD VARIATIONS

FROM SPICY HARISSA AND SMOKED VEGETABLES TO CRISPY PANCETTA, THESE IDEAS ARE SURE TO BE ENJOYED BY ALL THE FAMILY AS WELL AS BEING LIGHT AND HEALTHY TO EAT, TOO.

CAPRESE QUINOA COUSCOUS SALAD

In place of the burrata cheese, use 250 g (9 oz.) baby mozzarella balls. Cook the quinoa as in the main recipe on page 122 and spoon onto a large serving platter, then arrange 2 sliced plum tomatoes and the mozzarella balls over the top. Finish by scattering 1 tablespoon chopped fresh basil over the salad. Offer some extra dressing when serving: mix the juice of 1 lemon with 150 ml (5 fl oz.) extra-virgin olive oil and season to taste. Serve with sliced focaccia.

GOAT'S CHEESE AND ROCKET QUINOA COUSCOUS SALAD WITH PANCETTA

Cook the quinoa as in the main recipe. Fry 100 g (3½ oz.) smoked pancetta cubes (or lardons) in a frying pan until crisp, and set to one side. Loosely mix 125 g (4½ oz.) rocket leaves with the cooked quinoa. Spoon the cooked quinoa and rocket onto a serving platter, or divide between four plates and then scatter the cooked pancetta over the top. Sprinkle 150 g (5¼ oz.) crumbled goat's cheese over the salad and serve with crusty bread such as a baguette.

MOROCCAN QUINOA COUSCOUS SALAD WITH ROASTED VEGETABLES AND HARISSA

Roast the following vegetables together in 2 tablespoons olive oil in a preheated oven (200°C/400°F/Gas Mark 6) for 45 minutes until cooked and slightly charred: 1 aubergine, diced small; 2 courgettes, diced small; 1 large onion, peeled and cut into quarters; 3 large tomatoes, cut into small dice. Mix the roasted vegetables with the cooked quinoa, add 1 teaspoon harissa paste, and mix well. Season to taste with salt and black pepper. Serve warm with chopped fresh flat-leaf parsley sprinkled over the top, and warm pita bread.

ROCKET

Rocket has a wonderful peppery flavour and is easy to grow at home. Low in calories and high in antioxidants, this is truly a superfood that adds essential vitamins, minerals, taste and texture to all kinds of recipes. Like kale, this vegetable is high in vitamin C, which boosts immunity and helps the body fight infectious diseases. Scatter a handful of rocket leaves among other salad leaves or add them to steamed seasonal greens for extra taste and flavour.

QUINOA KISIR WITH POMEGRANATE AND WALNUTS

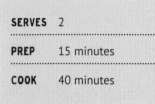

SERVES	2
PREP	15 minutes
COOK	40 minutes

YOU WILL NEED

2 tablespoons extra-virgin olive oil

1 small onion, peeled and chopped

2 garlic cloves, peeled and minced

1 teaspoon ground cumin

1 teaspoon allspice

1 teaspoon paprika

1 red chilli, seeded and finely chopped

1 tablespoon tomato purée

100 g (3½ oz.) uncooked black quinoa

2 tomatoes, cored and diced

4 spring onions, trimmed and sliced

50 g (2 oz.) pomegranate seeds

large handful of fresh flat-leaf parsley, leaves and stalks chopped

handful of fresh mint, leaves chopped

zest and juice of 1 lemon

1 tablespoon pomegranate molasses

60 g (2¼ oz.) walnut pieces

salt and black pepper

KISIR IS A TURKISH SALAD THAT'S SIMILAR TO TABBOULEH. FRESH FLAVOURS ARE KEY — HOT CHILLI, ZESTY LEMON AND PLENTY OF FRESH HERBS. BLACK QUINOA GIVES THIS LIGHT AND ZINGY DISH A CHEWY TEXTURE AND ADDS A BIT OF DRAMA.

1 Warm 1 tablespoon of the olive oil in a saucepan. Add the onion and season with salt and black pepper. Sweat over a low heat for 5–8 minutes, stirring every so often, until the onion is soft but hasn't coloured. If it starts to brown, turn the heat down.

2 Stir in the garlic, cumin, allspice, paprika, chilli and tomato purée. Cook and stir for 1–2 minutes until the mixture smells aromatic.

3 Add the quinoa to the saucepan with 240 ml (8 fl oz.) cold water. Cover. Bring to a boil, then turn the heat down and gently simmer for 20–25 minutes, or until all the water has been absorbed and the quinoa is tender. If it looks like it's getting too dry while it cooks, add a splash more water. Drain well.

4 Transfer the cooked quinoa to a bowl. Add the tomatoes, spring onions, pomegranate seeds, parsley and mint. Stir together.

5 Add the lemon zest to the bowl. Whisk the lemon juice with the remaining 1 tablespoon of olive oil, 1 tablespoon of pomegranate molasses, and some salt and black pepper. Stir into the salad. Taste and add more salt and pepper if you think it needs it.

6 Toast the walnut pieces in a dry frying pan over a low heat. Shake the pan to keep the walnut pieces moving and toast for 2–3 minutes, until they are golden brown. Stir the nuts into the kisir and serve.

FREE FROM
DAIRY, GLUTEN & WHEAT

COLOUR CHANGE
You can make this
salad with white
quinoa, if you prefer.
Remember, it takes
less time to cook than
black quinoa – around
10–15 minutes.

SUMMER QUINOA SALAD WITH GRAPEFRUIT AND TAHINI DRESSING

(VG)

SERVES	4
PREP	10 minutes
COOK	35 minutes

YOU WILL NEED

225 g (8 oz.) fresh asparagus

juice of ½ grapefruit (about 80 ml/3 fl oz.)

1 garlic clove, minced

2 tablespoons olive oil

1 tablespoon tahini

1 tablespoon maple syrup

150 g (5¼ oz.) fresh baby rocket leaves

250 g (9 oz.) halved red grapes

270 g (9½ oz.) cooked quinoa

60 g (2¼ oz.) dry-roasted hazelnuts, chopped

salt and black pepper

FREE FROM
DAIRY, GLUTEN & WHEAT

LAYERS OF FRESH FLAVOUR MAKE THIS BRIGHT CITRUSY SALAD WITH A PEPPERY BASE A SUMMERTIME STAPLE. THE DISH WORKS WITHOUT THE ASPARAGUS AS WELL, ALTHOUGH THE WARM TOPPER WORKS TO BRING OUT ITS FRAGRANT NOTES.

1 Preheat the oven to 180°C/350°F/Gas Mark 4.

2 Arrange the asparagus on a baking tray, drizzle with oil and sprinkle with salt. Roast in the oven for 30–35 minutes.

3 In a large bowl, whisk together the grapefruit juice, garlic, olive oil, tahini and maple syrup. Add the rocket, grapes, quinoa and hazelnuts, and toss with the dressing. Top with the warm asparagus, and season with salt and black pepper to taste.

FRUITY QUINOA TABBOULEH WITH FETA CHEESE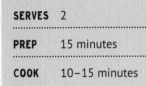

SERVES	2
PREP	15 minutes
COOK	10–15 minutes

YOU WILL NEED

50 g (2 oz.) uncooked quinoa

1 small red onion, peeled and diced

2 small tomatoes, cored and diced

very large handful of fresh flat-leaf parsley, leaves and stalks finely chopped

large handful of fresh mint, leaves finely chopped

20 g (¾ oz.) chopped dried apricots

70 g (2½ oz.) dried cranberries

15 g (½ oz.) chopped pistachios

zest and juice of 1 lemon

1 teaspoon allspice

2 tablespoons extra-virgin olive oil

115 g (4 oz.) crumbled feta cheese

salt and black pepper

FREE FROM
GLUTEN & WHEAT

GREEN WITH PARSLEY AND MINT, AND FLAVOURED WITH VIBRANT LEMON AND WARMING ALLSPICE, TABBOULEH MAKES A GREAT LIGHT MEAL — OR HAVE IT AS PART OF A MEZZE PLATTER FOR A MIDDLE EASTERN FEAST.

1 Put the quinoa in a saucepan with 120 ml (4 fl oz.) cold water. Cover. Bring to a boil, then turn the heat down and gently simmer for 10–15 minutes, or until all the water has been absorbed and the quinoa is tender. If it looks like it's getting too dry while it cooks, add a splash more water. Drain well.

2 Transfer the cooked quinoa to a bowl. Add the red onion, tomatoes, parsley, mint, apricots, cranberries and pistachios. Stir it all together until well combined.

3 Add the lemon zest to the tabbouleh with the allspice.

4 Whisk the lemon juice with the olive oil and some salt and black pepper, then stir into the tabbouleh. Taste and add more salt and pepper if you think it needs it.

5 Top the tabbouleh with the crumbled feta cheese for serving.

MEZZE PLANS: Combine with recipes on pages 68, 112 and 126 to build up a Levantine feast. Serve with some falafel and hummus.

RINSE FIRST
Feta is a brined cheese and normally comes sealed in a pouch with some brine to keep it from drying out. Give it a gentle rinse under cold water and pat dry with kitchen towel to reduce the salty flavour.

QUINOA TABBOULEH VARIATIONS
TABBOULEH IS AN EASY SALAD TO ADAPT TO WHAT'S IN SEASON OR IN YOUR FRIDGE. A MIX OF HERBS, GRAINS, GREENS AND SPICES IS ALL YOU NEED.

WINTER GREENS QUINOA TABBOULEH

Follow the main recipe on page 130 but swap the parsley and mint for blanched and shredded winter greens such as kale or cabbage, and use chopped walnuts instead of pistachios. To blanch the greens, bring a saucepan of water to a boil. Discard any thick stalks and finely shred the leaves, then add them to the saucepan of boiling water. Simmer for 2 minutes. Drain and rinse under cold water. Shake off any excess water and mix into the tabbouleh with the rest of the ingredients.

SICILIAN QUINOA TABBOULEH

Swap the mint for fresh basil and the cranberries for raisins per the main recipe. Use 1 teaspoon chilli flakes instead of the allspice and add toasted pine nuts instead of the pistachios along with 50 g (2 oz.) pitted green olives. Omit the feta cheese. Warm a dry frying pan, then put in the pine nuts. Toast for 2 minutes until the nuts are golden. They will toast very quickly and burn easily, so keep shaking the frying pan and don't take your eyes off the pine nuts while they're cooking.

FETA AND WATERMELON QUINOA TABBOULEH

Omit the dried apricots and cranberries per the main recipe. Stir in 310 g (11 oz.) peeled, chopped watermelon with 1 teaspoon ground cumin instead of the allspice.

FETA CHEESE

Greek feta – and only feta made in Greece can be called feta – is a tangy cheese that is made with sheep's milk and is a salad's best friend. Greek salad can't be made without it, but feta's crumbly texture and salty flavour also pairs well with fresh, crunchy vegetables. Try crumbling it over honey-roasted carrots, slices of sweet melon (especially watermelon), slices of juicy cucumber and tomatoes, ribbons of courgette, charred chunks of aubergine, into potato salads and coleslaws, or with wilted winter greens. It also cooks nicely in the oven. Sprinkle it on top of stuffed vegetables and bake until golden or wrap it in aluminium foil with fresh herbs, ground black pepper, lemon zest and a little olive oil and bake for 10–15 minutes at 180°C/350°F/Gas Mark 4 until soft. Serve with crudités for dipping.

BEETROOT AND CARROT QUINOA CAKES WITH CUMIN YOGHURT SAUCE

(V)

MAKES	18 cakes
PREP	20 minutes
COOK	30 minutes

YOU WILL NEED

1 tablespoon cumin seeds

180 g (6¼ oz.) cooked quinoa

1 beetroot, peeled and grated

2 carrots, peeled and grated

1 shallot, minced

15 g (½ oz.) chopped fresh coriander

1 teaspoon fine sea salt

2 eggs

60 g (2¼ oz.) plain flour

1 teaspoon baking powder

1 tablespoon olive oil, for frying

FOR THE SAUCE

140 g (5 oz.) plain Greek-style yoghurt

zest of 1 lime

1 tablespoon fresh lime juice

1 garlic clove, minced

½ teaspoon fine sea salt

½ teaspoon ground cumin

2 tablespoons chopped fresh coriander

pinch of ground cayenne pepper (optional)

THESE LITTLE CAKES ARE A HIT WITH FAMILY MEMBERS LARGE AND SMALL. PACKED WITH EARTHY, SWEET ROOT VEGETABLES, THEY'RE A GREAT EXAMPLE OF HOW QUINOA CAN MAKE A SUBTLE YET POWERFUL CONTRIBUTION TO A MEAL.

1 To make the sauce, combine all the ingredients in a small bowl and set it aside to rest while you make the quinoa cakes.

2 Place the cumin seeds in a frying pan over a medium–high heat. Toast for about 2 minutes, shaking the frying pan a few times, until very fragrant and lightly browned. Pour the seeds into a mixing bowl.

3 Add the quinoa, beetroot, carrot, shallot, coriander, salt and a few grinds of black pepper. Mix well. Clear some space on one side of the bowl and crack the eggs in. Beat thoroughly, then incorporate the eggs into the vegetable mixture. Sprinkle the flour and baking powder over the mixture then stir to incorporate.

4 Heat the olive oil over a medium–high heat until shimmering. Spoon about 60 ml (2 fl oz.) batter into the frying pan for each cake, gently spreading to form cakes about 6 mm (¼ in.) thick. Cook four or five cakes at a time so you don't crowd the frying pan. Cook for 4 minutes on the first side, then flip and cook for 3–4 minutes on the second side. You may need to adjust the heat so that the cakes brown nicely on the outside while cooking thoroughly on the inside.

5 Set the cooked cakes on a wire rack or kitchen towel-lined plate. Add a little more oil to the frying pan and continue cooking in batches until you've used all the batter. Serve warm or at room temperature with the cumin yoghurt sauce.

THAI-STYLE CRAB, POMELO AND QUINOA SALAD

SERVES	2
PREP	20 minutes
COOK	15–20 minutes

YOU WILL NEED

50 g (2 oz.) uncooked red quinoa

½ pomelo, peeled and the flesh picked from the membrane

4 shallots, peeled and finely sliced

large handful fresh coriander leaves

40 g (1½ oz.) raw peanuts

150 g (5¼ oz.) white crabmeat

1 mild red chilli, sliced

juice of 1 lime

1 tablespoon fish sauce

1½ tablespoons light soft brown sugar

salt

FREE FROM
DAIRY, GLUTEN & WHEAT

CITRUS AND SEAFOOD ALWAYS MAKE A GOOD MIX. INSPIRED BY HOT, SHARP, SWEET THAI SALADS, HERE JUICY POMELO IS PAIRED WITH DELICATE WHITE CRAB AND PLENTY OF CORIANDER.

1 Put the quinoa in a saucepan with 120 ml (4 fl oz.) cold water. Cover. Bring to a boil, then turn the heat right down and gently simmer for 15–20 minutes, or until all the water has been absorbed and the quinoa is tender. If it looks like it's getting too dry while it cooks, add a splash more water. Drain well.

2 Transfer the cooked quinoa to a bowl. Add the pomelo, shallots and coriander leaves and mix together.

3 Warm a dry frying pan over a medium heat. Put in the peanuts and cook, stirring, for 3–4 minutes until the nuts are golden brown and smell toasted. Turn them out of the frying pan, leave them to cool for a few minutes, then chop them roughly.

4 Arrange the quinoa on a couple of plates or one big serving plate. Top with the peanuts, crabmeat and sliced chilli.

5 Whisk the lime juice with the fish sauce and sugar. Taste and add a pinch of salt if it's needed. Drizzle over the salad for serving.

ROASTED WINTER VEGETABLE, QUINOA AND WILD RICE SALAD

(V)

SERVES	4–8
PREP	20 minutes
COOK	45 minutes

YOU WILL NEED

600 ml (20 fl oz.) good vegetable stock

1 teaspoon dried herbes de Provence

1 garlic clove, smashed

1 teaspoon fine sea salt

80 g (3 oz.) wild rice

100 g (3½ oz.) uncooked red quinoa

3 carrots, trimmed, peeled and cut into 2 cm (¾ in.) pieces

2 purple or golden beetroot, trimmed, peeled and cut into 2 cm (¾ in.) pieces

3 parsnips, trimmed, peeled and cut into 2 cm (¾ in.) pieces

1 tablespoon olive oil

20 g (¾ oz.) chopped fresh flat-leaf parsley

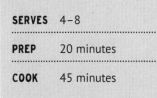

FREE FROM
DAIRY, GLUTEN & WHEAT

THIS HEARTY SALAD WORKS EQUALLY WELL AS A MAIN COURSE OR AS AN ACCOMPANIMENT TO OTHER DISHES. THE HINT OF ORANGE IN THE DRESSING BRINGS ALL OF THE FLAVOURS TOGETHER BEAUTIFULLY.

1 Preheat the oven to 200°C/400°F/Gas Mark 6.

2 In a covered medium pot, bring the stock to a boil with the herbes de Provence, garlic and ½ teaspoon of the salt (if the stock is unsalted). When it boils, add the wild rice, cover, reduce to a simmer, and cook for 30 minutes. Stir in the quinoa and simmer for a further 15 minutes. Remove from the heat and leave for 10 minutes before uncovering and fluffing with a fork.

3 Meanwhile, toss the root vegetables with the olive oil and the remaining salt on a rimmed baking tray big enough to accommodate them in a single layer without crowding. Roast in the centre of the oven, turning once or twice with a spatula, until browned on the outside and tender throughout, about 30 minutes.

4 To make the dressing, place the shallot in a small bowl, pour in the sherry vinegar and orange juice, and leave for 15 minutes. Then add the orange zest, honey, mustard, salt and pepper, and whisk to combine. Whisk in the olive oil.

5 Combine the rice and quinoa with the roasted vegetables in a large mixing bowl. While still warm, pour the dressing over the salad and toss gently. Stir in the parsley. Serve warm or at room temperature.

FOR THE DRESSING
I shallot, minced
I tablespoon sherry vinegar
I tablespoon fresh orange juice
½ teaspoon orange zest
½ teaspoon mild honey
½ teaspoon Dijon mustard
¼ teaspoon fine sea salt
a few good grinds of black pepper
2 tablespoons extra-virgin olive oil

BAKES & DESSERTS

FLUFFY AND FRUITY QUINOA SCONES

POWER BOOST SNICKERDOODLES

CHOCOLATE PEANUT BUTTER BARS

RICH AND FUDGY QUINOA BROWNIES

QUINOA CINNAMON POWER BITES

BLUEBERRY PISTACHIO QUINOA PARFAIT WITH QUINOA PRALINE

SPICED CASHEW 'CHEESECAKE' WITH RED QUINOA CRUST

ICED ORANGE, SEMOLINA AND QUINOA LAYER CAKE

APPLE CRUMBLE WITH QUINOA TOPPING

MULTISEED AND QUINOA BREAD

Recipe on page 152

FLUFFY AND FRUITY QUINOA SCONES

(V)

MAKES	12
PREP	5 minutes
COOK	10–15 minutes

YOU WILL NEED

180 g (6¼ oz.) quinoa
flour, plus more for rolling

80 g (3 oz.) coconut flour

80 g (3 oz.) cornmeal

½ teaspoon sea salt

1½ teaspoons baking
powder

½ teaspoon bicarbonate of
soda

50 g (2 oz.) sugar

85 g (3¼ oz.) unsalted
butter

150 g (5¼ oz.) mixed dried
fruit

zest of 1 large orange

120 ml (4 fl oz.) buttermilk

butter and preserves, for
serving

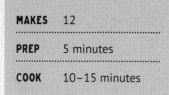

FREE FROM
GLUTEN & WHEAT

SERVE THESE FRUITY QUINOA SCONES WARM FROM THE OVEN WITH BUTTER, AND MAYBE SOME HONEY AND JAM FOR A SPECIAL WEEKEND BRUNCH. THEY ALSO MAKE A GREAT SNACK.

1 Preheat the oven to 220°C/425°F/Gas Mark 7, and line a large baking tray with baking paper.

2 Put all of the flours, the salt, baking powder, bicarbonate of soda and sugar in a mixing bowl, and rub in the butter with your fingers until the mixture resembles fine breadcrumbs.

3 Add the dried fruit and orange zest and mix well.

4 Make a well in the centre and pour in the buttermilk, then mix to incorporate all of the ingredients until you have a ball of dough. Don't overwork the dough or the scones will be tough.

5 Put the dough on a floured board and roll out to about 2.5 cm (1 in.) thickness. Stamp out 12 scones with a 5 cm (2 in.) cutter, then put them on the baking tray.

6 Bake for 10–15 minutes, until well risen and golden brown.

7 Serve warm with butter and preserves.

QUINOA SCONE VARIATIONS

SWEET AND SAVOURY SCONES WILL EASILY FIT IN TO ANY SCHOOL OR OFFICE LUNCHBOX AND ARE A CUTE CHOICE FOR PICNICS, TOO. THESE ADDITIONAL IDEAS TICK ALL THE TASTE AND CONVENIENCE BOXES FOR ALL OCCASIONS.

CRANBERRY AND BLUEBERRY WHOLEMEAL SCONES

Follow the main recipe on page 142 but use 160 g (5½ oz.) wholemeal flour in place of the coconut flour and cornmeal, and replace the mixed dried fruit with 140 g (5 oz.) dried cranberries and blueberries. Serve warm, split, and spread with butter for an afternoon treat.

MEXICAN CHEESE AND JALAPEÑO SAVOURY SCONES

Simply omit the coconut flour, sugar, dried fruit and orange zest in the main recipe, and in their place add an extra 80 g (3 oz.) cornmeal; 150 g (5¼ oz.) grated cheddar cheese; 3 tablespoons tinned jalapeño peppers, drained and finely chopped; and 1 teaspoon dried oregano. Make as per the main recipe, and bake for 10–15 minutes. Serve warm with butter, tomato salsa and salad, or with chilli, stews or soups.

PLAIN AMERICAN-STYLE BUTTERMILK BISCUITS

If you want a plain, light and crumbly breakfast treat, these are just right. Follow the main recipe but replace the coconut flour and cornmeal, with 160 g (5½ oz.) plain white flour. Omit the sugar, dried fruit and orange zest and add an extra ½ teaspoon of baking powder to the dry ingredients before rubbing in the butter and following the method as in on page 142. Serve alongside a cooked breakfast or use to make a breakfast sandwich. These are also excellent when used as a topping for a sweet or savoury American cobbler.

CRANBERRIES

Cranberries are billed as one of the world's healthiest foods. Acting as a strong barrier to bacteria, these ruby-red fruits pack a punch when it comes to the list of vitamins they contain – they are high in vitamins C, E and K, and are also a very good source of antioxidants and minerals. Dried cranberries can be scattered over cereal and porridge as well as being added to bakes, cakes and salads – there's no need to wait until Christmas to enjoy them.

POWER BOOST SNICKERDOODLES

MAKES	24
PREP	15 minutes, plus chilling
COOK	15 minutes

YOU WILL NEED

2 tablespoons freshly ground flaxseed

120 g (4¼ oz.) non-dairy butter

200 g (7 oz.) sugar

90 g (3¼ oz.) cooked quinoa

180 g (6¼ oz.) gluten-free plain flour

1 ½ teaspoons cream of tartar

1 teaspoon baking powder

½ teaspoon salt

1 ½ tablespoons ground cinnamon, for rolling

FREE FROM
DAIRY, GLUTEN
& WHEAT

QUINOA ADDS A PROTEIN BOOST TO THIS FAMILY FAVOURITE, CLASSIC COOKIE.

1 Combine the flaxseed with 80 ml (2¾ fl oz.) warm water and set aside (this creates a binding gel).

2 In a large mixing bowl, cream together the butter and 150 g (5¼ oz.) sugar. In a seperate bowl, mix together the flour, cream of tartar, baking powder, and salt. Pour the dry mixture into the bowl with the butter, sugar and quinoa and stir it all together until the dough comes together in a ball. Put the bowl of dough in the fridge to chill for about 1 hour.

3 Preheat the oven to 180°C/350°F/Gas Mark 4, and line a baking tray with baking paper.

4 Combine the remaining sugar with the ground cinnamon. When the dough has cooled, remove it from the fridge. Using your hands, roll the pieces of the dough into 2.5 cm (1 in.) balls, roll them through the cinnamon sugar, and place them on the baking tray. Use all the dough, and place the balls 5 cm (2 in.) apart on the baking tray.

5 Bake for 13–15 minutes.

6 Cool completely before storing in an airtight container. The cookies will keep for up to 1 week at room temperature or for 2 weeks in the fridge.

CHOCOLATE PEANUT BUTTER BARS

VG

MAKES	20–22
PREP	12 minutes, plus setting
COOK	5 minutes

YOU WILL NEED

180 g (6¼ oz.) pitted dried dates

90 g (3¼ oz.) raw cashew nuts

80 g (3 oz.) peanut butter

60 g (2¼ oz.) cooked quinoa

25 g (¾ oz.) almond meal

100 g (3 ½ oz.) organic dark chocolate (70% cocoa solids), chopped

FREE FROM DAIRY, GLUTEN & WHEAT

THESE CHOCOLATE-COVERED BARS ARE PACKED WITH PROTEIN AND FLAVOUR — AND YOU CAN ENJOY THEM ANY TIME! THIS DOUGH CAN ALSO BE FORMED INTO BALLS AND ROLLED THROUGH MELTED CHOCOLATE TO MAKE ELEGANT TRUFFLES.

1 Line a baking tray with baking paper.

2 Put the dates in a food processor or liquidizer, and pulse until crumbly. Remove the dates, then add the cashews to the food processor or liquidizer and pulse to a crumble. Combine the dates and cashews in a mixing bowl. Alternatively, chop the dates and cashews to a coarse crumb and combine.

3 Add the peanut butter, cooked quinoa and almond meal to the date and cashew mixture. Stir to combine.

4 Using your hands, form the dough into a rectangle shape on the baking tray, then use a rolling pin to smooth it into an even layer. Transfer to the fridge for about 4 hours, until set.

5 Once set, cut into individual bar shapes. Melt the chocolate in a small heatproof bowl set over a saucepan of gently simmering water. Once melted, dip one side of each bar into the chocolate, and return to the baking tray to set.

6 Serve immediately or store the bars in an airtight container in the fridge for 7–10 days.

PEANUT BUTTER BAR VARIATIONS

SWAP INGREDIENTS TO CREATE A RANGE OF DIFFERENT PROTEIN-PACKED BARS. MILD SUNFLOWER SEED BUTTER LETS SWEET BANANA CHIPS SHINE, WHILE ADDING WALNUTS PROVIDES POWERFUL NUTRIENTS THAT ARE SAID TO PROMOTE HEART AND BRAIN HEALTH.

VANILLA APRICOT BARS

Follow the main recipe on page 148, but replace the peanut butter with 80 g (3 oz.) sunflower seed butter, replace the dates with 160 g (5½ oz.) chopped dried apricots, and replace the almond meal with 25 g (¾ oz.) vanilla protein powder.

BANANA CRUNCH BARS

Follow the main recipe, but replace 30 g (1 oz.) of the cashews with banana chips, and replace the peanut butter with sunflower seed butter.

COCONUT WALNUT BARS

Follow the main recipe, but replace the cashew nuts with walnuts, add 15 g (½ oz.) grated fresh coconut and ½ teaspoon of salt and combine with the dates.

NUT BUTTERS

The popularity of nut butters has exploded in recent years – people love the fact that they are so easy to make at home! Packed with heart healthy 'good' fats, essential proteins, vitamins and minerals, nut butters are a delicious way to get your daily nutrients. The recipe ideas are endless – keep it savoury by stirring a nut butter into a spicy soup or a Thai-inspired noodle dish. Sweets like cookies, energy bars and truffles always welcome a nut butter infusion. And this combination of nut butter and chocolate? A classic!

RICH AND FUDGY QUINOA BROWNIES

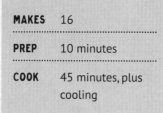

MAKES	16
PREP	10 minutes
COOK	45 minutes, plus cooling

YOU WILL NEED

spray oil or butter, for greasing

175 g (6 oz.) chocolate (60% cocoa solids), chopped

115 g (4 oz.) butter, diced

150 g (5¼ oz.) sugar

130 g (4¾ oz.) light brown sugar

3 eggs

190 g (6¾ oz.) cooked quinoa

1 tablespoon vanilla extract

½ teaspoon fine sea salt

3 tablespoons cornflour

30 g (1 oz.) cocoa powder

120 g (4¼ oz.) chopped walnuts or pecans (optional)

FREE FROM
GLUTEN & WHEAT

THESE BROWNIES ARE INDULGENT, WITH THAT COVETED SHINY, CRACKLY LAYER ON TOP. YOU'D NEVER GUESS THAT THEY CONTAIN QUINOA AND ARE GLUTEN-FREE.

1 Preheat the oven to 180°C/350°F/Gas Mark 4 with a rack in the centre. Line the bottom and sides of a 20 cm (8 in.) square baking tin with aluminium foil, and butter the foil or spray with oil.

2 Put the chocolate and the butter in a large microwave-safe bowl. Heat at medium power for about 90 seconds and then in 30-second bursts if necessary, stirring well between heatings to incorporate any unmelted bits. Alternatively, melt the chocolate and butter together in a bowl set over a pan of simmering water, stirring frequently.

3 Add the white and brown sugars. Stir vigorously with a rubber spatula or wooden spoon until the sugar is well incorporated.

4 Put the eggs, quinoa, vanilla and salt in a liquidizer. Sift in the cornflour and cocoa powder. Blend the mixture until it's completely smooth, about 1 minute.

5 Pour the egg mixture into the bowl with the chocolate mixture. Stir vigorously for 2–3 minutes, until the batter is shiny and smooth. Mix in the chopped nuts, if using.

6 Pour the batter into the prepared baking tin. Gently tap it on the counter a few times to remove any air bubbles. Bake for 45 minutes.

7 Leave to cool for 10 minutes on a rack, then lift the brownies out of the tin using the foil, and leave to cool completely in the foil on a rack. Don't rush the cooling process or the brownies will be difficult to cut. Gently peel the foil off the brownies and, using a long, thin knife dipped in hot water and wiped with a kitchen towel between cuts, cut the brownie into 16 (5 cm/2 in.) squares.

EASY LINER
A great way to line the baking tin with foil is to turn the tin upside down, cut a square of foil from the roll, and mould the foil to the outside of the tin. Carefully remove the foil, then turn the tin right side up and press the foil into the tin.

QUINOA CINNAMON POWER BITES

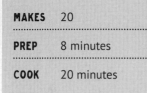

MAKES	20
PREP	8 minutes
COOK	20 minutes

YOU WILL NEED

1 tin (400 g/14 oz.) chickpeas, drained and rinsed

90 g (3¼ oz.) cooked quinoa

65 g (2¼ oz.) sugar

25 g (¾ oz.) almond flour

80 g (3 oz.) almond butter

1 tablespoon ground cinnamon

½ tablespoon cardamom

FREE FROM
DAIRY, GLUTEN & WHEAT

THIS MAKE-AHEAD RECIPE IS A PERFECT ON-THE-GO BREAKFAST BITE OR GO-TO WORKOUT SNACK. GROUP THE BITES IN BAGS OF THREE, AND ENJOY WITH A BREAKFAST SMOOTHIE OR AS AN AFTERNOON PICK-ME-UP.

1 In a food processor, pulse the chickpeas until crumbly, about 1 minute. Add the cooked quinoa, sugar and almond flour and pulse to combine, about 30 seconds. Scrape down the sides of the bowl with a spatula. Add the almond butter, cinnamon and cardamom, and process until a dough ball forms.

2 Transfer the dough ball to a clean bowl and put it in the fridge.

3 Heat the oven to 180°C/350°F/Gas Mark 4, and line a baking tray with baking paper. Once the oven has reached the correct temperature, remove the dough from the fridge. Use a tablespoon to scoop out golf-ball-size pieces and then roll them into balls using your hands. Place the balls on the baking tray and repeat until you've used up all of the dough.

4 Bake for 20 minutes, or until the bites are cooked through.

NO-BAKE BITES
These snacks can also be made without baking. Simply place the balls on the baking tray in the fridge to set. Transfer to an airtight container and store in the fridge for up to 1 week.

POWER BITE VARIATIONS
TRY ADDING THE BRIGHT, TART FLAVOUR OF CITRUS FRUIT OR DRIED CHERRIES TO YOUR POWER BITES — OR MIX IN CHOCOLATE AND WALNUTS FOR ADDED DEPTH.

(V) (DF) (GF) (WF)

CHOCOLATE CRUNCH POWER BITES
To the chickpeas, cooked quinoa, sugar, almond butter and almond flour, add 75 g (2½ oz.) vegan chocolate chips and 40 g (1½ oz.) chopped walnuts. Leave out the cinnamon and cardamon.

(V) (DF) (GF) (WF)

TART CHERRY POWER BITES
To the chickpeas, cooked quinoa, sugar and almond flour, add 80 g (3 oz.) sunflower seed butter in place of the almond butter, 75 g (2½ oz.) dried cherries and the zest of 1 lemon. Omit the cinnamon and cardamon.

(V) (DF) (GF) (WF)

SUMMER CITRUS POWER BITES
To the chickpeas, cooked quinoa, sugar and almond flour, add 80 g (3 oz.) sunflower seed butter, 2–3 drops pure orange extract and the zest of 2 lemons.

CINNAMON

Cinnamon is a spice that has long been renowned for its medicinal properties, from heart health to blood sugar control. To gain the benefits of cinnamon, add it to more of your foods: stir it into your chilli for a hint of spice, sprinkle it into your coffee for a warming spike, top your morning porridge, or dust over a slice of peanut butter toast. For something lighter, you could add it to a bowl of fresh fruit or swirl it into a serving of creamy yoghurt.

BLUEBERRY PISTACHIO QUINOA PARFAIT WITH QUINOA PRALINE

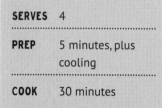

SERVES	4
PREP	5 minutes, plus cooling
COOK	30 minutes

FOR THE CREAMY QUINOA

200 g (7 oz.) uncooked tricolour quinoa

600 ml (20 fl oz.) non-dairy milk

6 tablespoons maple syrup

1 teaspoon vanilla extract

60 g (2¼ oz.) chia seeds

FOR THE QUINOA PRALINE

60 g (2¼ oz.) uncooked tricolour quinoa

3 tablespoons sugar

3 tablespoons light brown sugar

¾ teaspoon vanilla extract

1½ tablespoons coconut oil

1½ tablespoons non-dairy milk

pinch of salt

FOR THE FILLINGS

150 g (5¼ oz.) fresh blueberries

60 g (2¼ oz.) roasted salted pistachios

FREE FROM
DAIRY, GLUTEN & WHEAT

THIS FANCY DESSERT IS AS DELECTABLE AS IT IS GORGEOUS. BRIGHT, CREAMY QUINOA PROVIDES AN EXCELLENT CANVAS FOR FRESH BLUEBERRIES AND GREEN PISTACHIOS. THE GAME-CHANGER HERE, THOUGH, IS THE BEAUTIFUL TRICOLOUR QUINOA PRALINE.

1 To make the creamy quinoa, put all of the ingredients, except for the chia seeds, in a large saucepan. Cover partially with a lid and simmer over a medium–low heat for 20 minutes, or until the quinoa is soft. There will be excess liquid.

2 Stir the chia seeds into the creamy quinoa, transfer to a bowl, and refrigerate for 1 hour, or until chilled.

3 To make the praline, while the creamy quinoa is cooling, warm a frying pan over a medium heat. Once hot, add the quinoa to the frying pan and move the seeds around occasionally so that they do not burn.

4 Once the quinoa starts to pop, cover the saucepan with a lid and continue to keep the seeds moving for 5–10 minutes. Lower the heat if the quinoa starts to smoke heavily. Popping quinoa should have a similar aroma to popping corn.

(continued)

5 When the quinoa has darkened slightly and smells toasted, set the frying pan aside. Place the quinoa and the rest of the praline ingredients in a saucepan and warm, covered, over a medium heat.

6 Line a baking tray with baking parchment or a silicone mat. Bring the praline mixture to a boil, stirring often, and making sure none of the sugar crystals are missed. Cook until all sugar is dissolved and test the texture by dropping a tiny amount into a glass of cold water; when picked out, it should be soft and flexible.

7 Take the saucepan off the hob and stir vigorously until the praline pulls away from the sides of the saucepan. Place 8 spoonfuls onto the baking tray and cool for 10 minutes.

8 Get four short, wide glasses out. Make a parfait by spooning 5 tablespoons creamy quinoa into a glass, then 2 tablespoons blueberries, 1 tablespoon pistachios, and one round of crumbled praline, then repeat for a second round of everything and top with intact praline instead of crumbled. Do this for all the glasses and serve chilled.

QUINOA PARFAIT VARIATIONS
AS PERFECT AS THIS BEAUTIFUL BLUEBERRY PISTACHIO DESSERT IS, THERE ARE CERTAINLY WAYS TO TRY OUT AN ASSORTMENT OF PREPARATIONS AND FLAVOURS WHILE KEEPING IT CLASSY.

APPLE AND CASHEW
If you don't like blueberries or pistachios, try using diced Fuji or Gala apples and roasted cashews instead. Add ½ teaspoon ground cinnamon to the creamy quinoa to pair with the apples for this variation.

PARTY PARFAIT
You can easily make this recipe fit for a party by preparing it in a large trifle dish instead of individual glasses.

MINT CHOCOLATE
Make a mint chocolate version of this parfait by adding ¼ teaspoon mint extract to the creamy quinoa after it has finished cooking, and using 150 g (5¼ oz.) chopped dark chocolate (70 per cent cocoa solids) in place of the blueberries.

SPICED CASHEW 'CHEESECAKE' WITH RED QUINOA CRUST

RED QUINOA MAKES A GREAT SUBSTITUTE FOR DIGESTIVE BISCUITS OR FLOUR IN THIS CHEESECAKE CRUST. THE QUINOA FLOUR GIVES IT A GREAT CRUNCH AND A DISTINCT FLAVOUR THAT PAIRS PERFECTLY WITH THE CREAMY CHEESECAKE FILLING.

SERVES	6
PREP	5 minutes, plus soaking and cooling
COOK	30 minutes

YOU WILL NEED
240 g (8½ oz.) raw cashews

60 ml (2 fl oz.) melted unrefined coconut oil

3 tablespoons maple syrup

2 tablespoons lemon juice

2 tablespoons water

2 teaspoons ground cinnamon

1½ teaspoons vanilla extract

FOR THE CRUST
100 g (3½ oz.) uncooked red quinoa

3 tablespoons unrefined coconut oil

3 tablespoons coconut sugar

1 teaspoon minced fresh root ginger

pinch of ground nutmeg

pinch of salt

FREE FROM DAIRY, GLUTEN & WHEAT

1 Preheat the oven to 180°C/350°F/Gas Mark 4, and lightly grease a 15 cm (6 in.) spring-form tin with coconut oil.

2 Start by making the crust. Rinse and dry the red quinoa, then, put it in a food processor and pulse until it has a sand-like texture, similar to almond meal.

3 Add the coconut oil, coconut sugar, ginger, nutmeg and salt to the processor and pulse until evenly combined. Firmly press the crust mixture into the bottom of the spring-form tin.

4 Bake for 5 minutes, then set the tin on a cooling rack and leave until it has fully cooled. Once it is at room temperature, place the cake in the fridge to firm up.

5 While the crust is cooling, soak the cashews in a bowl of hot water for 20–30 minutes, or until soft. Drain and rinse.

6 Put the cashews and the filling ingredients into a high-speed liquidizer and purée until very smooth. Pour the filling into the spring-form tin and tap it down on a stable surface to spread it evenly and remove major air bubbles.

7 Bake the cheesecake for 20–25 minutes, or until the edges have browned and pulled away from the sides of the tin slightly. The cheesecake will not jiggle much. Let the cheesecake cool on a cooling rack, then refrigerate for at least 4–6 hours. Served chilled.

PRESS IT DOWN
Use a flat-bottomed
measuring cup or
glass to help press the
crust evenly into the
spring-form tin.

ICED ORANGE, SEMOLINA AND QUINOA LAYER CAKE

(V)

SERVES	12
PREP	5 minutes
COOK	30 minutes

YOU WILL NEED
180 g (6¼ oz.) cooked
    quinoa
180 g (6¼ oz.) cooked
    semolina
4 eggs
zest and juice of 2 oranges
180 ml (6 fl oz.) coconut oil
2 teaspoons baking powder
½ teaspoon salt

FOR THE ICING
1 tin (400 ml/14 fl oz.) full-
    fat coconut milk,
    refrigerated overnight
100 g (3½ oz.) icing sugar
zest of 1 orange, plus extra
    for topping

FREE FROM
DAIRY, GLUTEN
& WHEAT

THIS BEAUTIFUL CAKE IS DAIRY-FREE, AS IT USES COCONUT OIL IN THE SPONGE AS WELL AS FOR THE ICING! IT'S A FABULOUS SHOW-STOPPING CAKE FOR ANY SPECIAL OCCASION.

1 Preheat the oven to 180°C/350°F/Gas Mark 4. Use the butter or spray to grease two 20 cm (8 in.) cake tins, and then line with parchment.

2 Put the quinoa, semolina, eggs, zest and juice, coconut oil, baking powder, and salt in a large mixing bowl and beat with a hand mixer for 2 minutes. Adjust the thickness if too liquid with a little more quinoa or semolina – the consistency should be like a very thick batter.

3 Divide the cake mixture between the two tins and bake for 30 minutes, until risen and golden brown.

4 Let the cake cool in the tins for 2 minutes, then turn out onto a wire rack to cool completely.

5 To make the icing: whip the coconut milk with the icing sugar and orange zest until light and fluffy. Put the icing in the fridge to thicken.

6 To decorate the cake, spread half of the icing over one cake and and add the other layer on top, positioning it so the edges align. Swirl the remaining icing over the top and sides of the cake, and decorate with a little extra orange zest.

7 Slice the cake and serve.

APPLE CRUMBLE WITH QUINOA TOPPING

(V)

SERVES	8
PREP	20 minutes
COOK	1 hour 20 minutes

YOU WILL NEED

1.3 kg (3 lb.) apples

1 tablespoon lemon juice

65 g (2¼ oz.) sugar

3 tablespoons plain flour

1 teaspoon ground cinnamon

¼ teaspoon ground nutmeg

⅛ teaspoon fine sea salt

FOR THE TOPPING

100 g (3½ oz.) uncooked quinoa

75 g (2½ oz.) rolled oats

130 g (4¾ oz.) light brown sugar

90 g (3¼ oz.) plain flour

115 g (4 oz.) butter, diced

vanilla cream, for serving

TRY A MIX OF GRANNY SMITH APPLES AND A SWEETER BAKING APPLE SUCH AS PINK LADY OR HONEYCRISP FOR THIS DESSERT. ANY APPLE PIE VARIETY WILL WORK WELL.

1 Preheat the oven to 190°C/375°F/Gas Mark 5 with a rack in the centre. While the oven heats, spread the quinoa on a rimmed baking tray and dry in the oven for 10 minutes. Pour into a small mixing bowl and set aside to cool.

2 To make the filling, peel, core and slice the apples into 6 mm (¼ in.) thick slices. Put them in a large mixing bowl and toss with the lemon juice. Sprinkle the sugar, flour, cinnamon, nutmeg and salt onto the apples and toss gently until the apples are evenly coated.

3 To make the topping, to the bowl with the quinoa, add and toss together the oats, brown sugar and flour. Add the diced butter and use your fingers to pinch the butter into the quinoa mixture until it forms a coarse crumble with no loose bits of dry ingredients.

4 Place a deep-dish pie tin or a 1.2 litre ovenproof dish onto a baking tray to catch any drips. Pour the apple mixture into the dish and sprinkle evenly with the crumble topping.

5 Bake until the filling is soft and bubbly and the topping is nicely browned, 65–75 minutes, covering loosely with aluminium foil when the topping is golden brown (around the 45-minute mark). Leave to cool for 10 minutes, and serve warm with vanilla cream.

EASY GLUTEN-FREE
For a gluten-free
version, use gluten-
free oats, substitute
the flour in the topping
with gluten-free flour,
and replace the flour
in the filling with
2 tablespoons
cornflour.

FRUIT CRUMBLE VARIATIONS

AT HEART, A CRUMBLE IS A FLEXIBLE DESSERT THAT HIGHLIGHTS SEASONAL FRUIT AND HELPS YOU DEAL WITH BUMPER CROPS. HERE ARE A COUPLE OF WAYS TO INCORPORATE SPRING AND SUMMER PRODUCE INTO THIS RECIPE.

BLUEBERRY CRUMBLE

For the filling, replace the apples with 1.3 kg (3 lb.) fresh or frozen blueberries. Reduce the sugar to 50 g (2 oz.) and swap in 2 tablespoons cornflour for the flour. Omit the cinnamon and nutmeg.

STRAWBERRY RHUBARB CRUMBLE

For the filling, replace the apples with 450 g (1 lb.) chopped fresh rhubarb stalks and 450 g (1 lb.) hulled, halved strawberries. Increase the sugar to 120 g (4¼ oz.). Swap in 2 tablespoons cornflour for the flour. Replace the cinnamon and nutmeg with 2 teaspoons vanilla extract.

INDIVIDUAL CRUMBLES

What could be better than having a sweet little dessert all to yourself? Instead of a large baking dish, divide the filling between eight oven-safe, 225 g (8 oz.) ramekins (or 300 ml/10 fl oz. jars) placed on a rimmed baking tray. Divide the topping in the same fashion. Bake for about 40 minutes, until browned and bubbly.

FREEZE IT: If you opt for 300 ml (10 fl oz.) jars, you can screw on the lids and freeze these little beauties, unbaked, for up to a few months, then uncover and put them all — or just one — into the oven when you need a little treat. Add a few minutes of baking time when baking from frozen. This version works with the original recipe and both flavour variations.

RHUBARB

For many fans of farmers' markets, the annual arrival of rhubarb signals a delicious new realm of possibilities. Rhubarb inspires childhood memories of harvesting stalks from the garden and dipping them in sugar to cut their bracing tartness. Though it can be used in savoury dishes, rhubarb is most often incorporated into baked goods and desserts – a grown-up version of dipping in sugar. It's low in calories and high in vitamins A, B and K, fibre and antioxidants. One thing to watch: the leaves are toxic, so if you grow rhubarb or buy it with leaves attached, be sure to remove them before heading into the kitchen.

MULTISEED AND QUINOA BREAD

(V)

MAKES	1 large loaf
PREP	1 hour 10 minutes
COOK	45 minutes

YOU WILL NEED

180 g (6¼ oz.) cooked quinoa

450 g (1 lb.) strong, white bread flour, plus extra for kneading

75 g (2½ oz.) oats

1 tablespoon sunflower seeds

1 tablespoon chia seeds

1 tablespoon flaxseed

1 teaspoon sea salt

1 packet (7 g/¼ oz.) instant yeast

60 ml (2 fl oz.) milk

180 ml (6 fl oz.) warm water

3 tablespoons olive oil

3 tablespoons honey

THIS FLUFFY QUINOA BREAD IS PACKED WITH ASSORTED SEEDS THAT GIVE IT A WONDERFULLY NUTTY TASTE AND TEXTURE. IT MAKES GREAT SANDWICHES AND IS FABULOUS TOASTED, TOO.

1 Put the cooked and cooled quinoa in a large mixing bowl and add the bread flour, oats, mixed seeds and the sea salt. Mix, and make a well in the centre of the ingredients.

2 Add the yeast to the mixture and pour the milk and warm water into the well – mix the liquids in, then add the olive oil and honey, and mix well again with your hands.

3 Turn the dough out onto a floured board and knead for 10 minutes until smooth and elastic. (You can use a food mixer with a dough hook to knead the dough if you wish.)

4 Put the dough in a bowl, cover, and leave to rise in a warm spot until doubled in size (about 1 hour).

5 Turn the dough out onto a floured board, knock it back, knead again, and then shape it to fit in a well-greased 900 g (2 lb.) loaf tin. Leave to rise once more until doubled in size, about 45 minutes.

6 Preheat the oven to 200°C/400°F/Gas Mark 6, and place a bowl of water in the bottom of the oven.

7 Bake the bread for 35–45 minutes; the bread is cooked when it is crusty, golden brown and sounds hollow when tapped underneath.

8 Let the bread cool for 15 minutes in the loaf tin before turning it out onto a wire cooling rack. Slice for serving. The bread can be used for sandwiches, toast, toasted cheese or simply buttered.

A

apple
   & cashew parfait 161
   apple pie crêpes 39
   crumble with quinoa
     topping 166–8
   spiced apple granola 34
artichoke & rocket dip 56
aubergine
   & quinoa dip 58
   pizza with blue cheese & 82

B

bacon, tomato & egg, muffins 46
banana crunch bars 150
bars 148–50
bean
   & butternut burger 94
   & chilli burritos 53
   & vegetable chilli 104
   burger with basil aïoli 92
   cauliflower quinoa soup 119
   cheesy quinoa bites 62–4
   pumped-up five-layer dip 60
   lettuce wraps 70
beetroot
   & carrot quinoa cakes 134–5
   roasted vegetable rice salad 138
berries 43
   & ricotta crêpes 38
   & summer fruit porridge 30
   waffles & berry compote 40–1
bhelpuri, puffed quinoa 66
biscuits, plain American-style
   buttermilk 144
blueberry
   & cranberry scones 144
   & lemon breakfast pudding 26
   crumble 168
   pistachio parfait 158–60

bread, multiseed 170
breakfast pudding 24–6
broccoli-cheddar bites 64–5
brownies 152
bulgur wheat 115
burgers, quinoa 92–4
burritos 51–3
butternut & bean burger 94–5

C

cacao quinoa protein shake 22
cardamom 35
   cardamom rose pudding 26
   vanilla cardamom granola 32
carrot
   & beetroot quinoa cakes 134–5
   roasted vegetable & wild rice
     salad 138
cauliflower quinoa soup 118
cheese
   bean & vegetable chilli 104
   broccoli-cheddar bites 64
   hot sauce quinoa bites 62
   caprese couscous salad 124
   cheddar & chive frittatas 48
   cheese & jalapeño scones 144
   couscous with blood oranges &
     burrata 122
   crêpes with berries & ricotta 38
   feta & spinach muffins 44
   goat's cheese & rocket couscous
     salad with pancetta 124
   ham & cheddar muffins 46
   Hawaiian cheesy pizza 84
   herby cream cheese &
     spring onion muffins 46
   individual margherita pizzas 84
   maple cream waffles 42
   nacho platter 72

   pizza with blue cheese &
     aubergine 82
   pizza bites 64
   roasted red pepper & goat's
     cheese frittatas 50
   shallot & Gruyère frittatas 50
   spicy meat feast pizza 84
   sun-dried tomato & mozzarella
     frittatas 50
   tabbouleh with feta 130–3
'cheesecake', spiced cashew 162
cherry
   & dark chocolate granola 34
   tart cherry power bites 156
chicken
   smoky Spanish quinoa with
     chorizo 110
   temaki sushi 91
chickpeas
   chickpea scramble burrito 51
   paella with chorizo & 100
   power bites 154–6
chilli, black bean & vegetable 104
chipotle sweet potato enchiladas 102
chirashi bowl 86–8
chocolate
   & cacao nib crêpes 39
   & cherry granola 34
   brownies 152
   crunch power bites 156
   mint parfait 161
   peanut butter bars 148
   waffles 42
chorizo
   & chickpea paella 100
   smoky Spanish quinoa 110–11
   spicy meat feast pizza 84
cinnamon power bites 154–5, 157
citrus power bites 156

coconut
    breakfast pudding 24
    curry squash bisque 120–1
    walnut bars 150
couscous salads 122–4
crab
    cakes 78
    Thai-style salad 136
cranberry & blueberry scones 144–5
crêpes 38–9
curry squash bisque 120–1

D
dips
    artichoke & rocket 56
    pumped-up five-layer 60
    smoky aubergine & quinoa 58
dumplings, spicy peanut veggie
    stew 96

E
eggs 47
    mini frittatas 48–50
    temaki sushi 91
    tomato, egg & bacon muffins 46
    vegetable paella 100
enchiladas, chipotle sweet
    potato 102

F
fish
    chirashi sushi bowl 86–8
    fish finger sandwich 74
    temaki sushi 89–91
frittatas, mini 48–50
fruity quinoa scones 142

G
ginger 73

maple sesame ginger breakfast
    pudding 26
granola, quinoa 32–4

H
ham
    & cheddar muffins 46
    spicy meat feast pizza 84
harissa vegetables, couscous
    salad 124
hot sauce quinoa bites 62

J
jalapeño pepper bites 64

K
kibbeh 68
kisir with pomegranate &
    walnuts 126–7

L
lamb quinoa meatballs 112–15
layer cake, iced 164
lentil burgers, lemon 94
lettuce wraps 70–2

M
maple syrup
    maple cream waffles 42
    maple sesame ginger breakfast
        pudding 26
meatballs 112–15
muffins, breakfast 44–6
mushrooms
    grilled veggie quinoa rolls with
        Cajun tahini sauce 76
    risotto with caramelized
        onions 106–8
    spicy peanut veggie stew with
        dumplings 96

temaki sushi 91

N
nacho platter 72
nuts 31
    brownies 152
    chocolate peanut butter bars 148
    coconut walnut bars 150
    granola 32–4
    kisir with pomegranate &
        walnuts 126–7
    maple cream waffles 42
    nut butters 151
    parfait with praline 158–61
    pecan quinoa porridge 28
    porridge with honey & almonds 29
    spiced cashew 'cheesecake' 162
    spicy peanut veggie stew with
        dumplings 96

O
oats
    fruit crumble with quinoa
        topping 166–8
    porridge with pecans & apricots 30
orange
    citrus power bites 156
    couscous with blood oranges &
        burrata 122
    layer cake 164

P
paella-style quinoa 98–100
pancakes, quinoa 36
parfait & quinoa praline 158–61
peach & nectarine waffles 42
pepper
    roasted, & goat's cheese
        frittatas 50

lettuce wraps 70
pizza, quinoa 82–4
   cheesy pizza bites 64
pomegranate & walnuts, kisir 126–7
pomelo 136–7
porridge, quinoa 28–30
prawn
   seafood paella 100
   temaki sushi 91
puffed (popped) quinoa 66

Q
quinoa
   cooking 18
   flour 12
   freezing 18
   puffing 66
   sprouting 91

R
rhubarb & strawberry crumble 168–9
rice & roasted vegetable salad 138–9
risotto-style quinoa 106–9
rocket 56, 125

S
saffron 101
salads
   couscous, blood oranges &
     burrata 122
   couscous with harissa
     vegetables 124
   feta & watermelon tabbouleh 132
   fruity tabbouleh with feta 130–2
   goat's cheese & rocket couscous
     with pancetta 124
   kisir with pomegranate &
     walnuts 126–7

roasted vegetable & wild rice
  138–9
   Sicilian tabbouleh 132
   summer, with grapefruit and
     tahini dressing 128
   Thai-style crab, pomelo &
     quinoa 136
   winter greens tabbouleh 132
scones
   cranberry & blueberry 144
   fluffy & fruity 142
   Mexican cheese & jalapeño 144
   plain American-style buttermilk
     biscuits 144
scramble, quinoa 51–3
seafood
   paella-style quinoa 100
   smoky Spanish quinoa with
     chorizo 111
shake, cacao protein 22
snickerdoodles, power boost 146
soups
   autumnal pumpkin 119
   curry squash bisque 120–1
   roasted cauliflower 118
   sourdough bread bowl 119
spinach
   & feta cheese muffins 44
   chickpea scramble burrito 51
sprouted quinoa 91
   chirashi sushi bowl 86–8
   temaki sushi 89–91
strawberry 43
   & apricot granola 34
   & rhubarb crumble 168
   compote, spiced, & pancakes 36
   summer fruit & berries porridge 30
sushi

chirashi bowl 86–8
temaki sushi 89–91
sweet potato
   & chipotle enchiladas 102
   bean & vegetable chilli 104
   quinoa kibbeh 68

T
tabbouleh 130–3
taco shells 72
tahini 27, 76, 128
tofu
   chirashi sushi bowl 88
   quinoa scramble 53
   temaki sushi 91
tomato 85
   caprese couscous salad 124
   chirashi sushi bowl 88
   pumped-up five-layer dip 60
   quinoa pizzas 82–4
   sun-dried tomato & mozzarella
     frittatas 50
   tomato, egg & bacon muffins 46
   vegetable paella 98–100
tortilla chips
   artichoke & rocket dip 56
   nacho platter 72
tortillas 51–3

V
vanilla
   & apricot bars 150
   & cardamom granola 32

W
waffles 40–2
watermelon & feta tabbouleh 132

RECIPE LIST BY BLOGGER

Karen S. Burns-Booth

Pecan Quinoa Porridge 28

Quinoa, Feta Cheese and Spinach Breakfast Muffins 44

Smoky Aubergine and Quinoa Dip 58

Quinoa-Coated Fish Finger Sandwich 74

Quinoa Crab Cakes 78

Quinoa Pizza with Blue Cheese and Aubergine 82

Quinoa Couscous with Blood Oranges and Burrata 122

Fluffy and Fruity Quinoa Scones 142

Iced Orange, Semolina and Quinoa Layer Cake 164

Multiseed and Quinoa Bread 170

Carolyn Cope

Vanilla Cardamom Quinoa Granola 32

Quinoa Pancakes with Spiced Strawberry Compote
    and Yoghurt 36

Quinoa, Cheddar and Chive Mini Frittatas 48

Vegetable Paella-Style Quinoa 98

Black Bean, Quinoa and Vegetable Chilli 104

Risotto-Style Quinoa with Caramelized Onions
    and Mushrooms 106

Beetroot and Carrot Quinoa Cakes with Cumin Yoghurt
    Sauce 134

Roasted Winter Vegetable, Quinoa and Wild Rice
    Salad 138

Rich and Fudgy Quinoa Brownies 152

Apple Crumble with Quinoa Topping 166

Jassy Davis

Quinoa Crêpes with Berries and Ricotta 38

Puffed Quinoa Bhelpuri 66

Sweet Potato Quinoa Kibbeh 68

Sprouted Quinoa Chirashi Sushi Bowl 86

Sprouted Quinoa and Salmon Temaki Sushi 89

Smoky Spanish Quinoa with Chicken and Chorizo 110

Lamb and Quinoa Meatballs 112

Quinoa Kisir with Pomegranate and Walnuts 126

Fruity Quinoa Tabbouleh with Feta Cheese 130

Thai-Style Crab, Pomelo and Quinoa Salad 136

Kristina Sloggett

Toasted Coconut and Quinoa Breakfast Pudding 24

Pumped-Up Five-Layer Quinoa Dip 60

Cheesy Hot Sauce Quinoa Bites 62

Quinoa Bean Burger with Basil Aïoli 92

Spicy Peanut Veggie Stew with Quinoa Dumplings 96

Chipotle Sweet Potato Quinoa Enchiladas 102

Summer Quinoa Salad with Grapefruit and
    Tahini Dressing 128

Power Boost Snickerdoodles 146

Chocolate Peanut Butter Bars 148

Quinoa Cinnamon Power Bites 154

Jackie Sobon

Cacao Quinoa Protein Shake 22

Quinoa Waffles with Berry Compote 40

Quinoa Chickpea Scramble Burrito 51

Quinoa-Dusted Tortilla Chips with Artichoke and
    Rocket Dip 56

Quinoa Lettuce Wraps 70

Grilled Veggie and Quinoa Summer Rolls with Cajun
    Tahini Sauce 76

Roasted Cauliflower Quinoa Soup 118

Curry Squash Quinoa Bisque with Coconut Cream 120

Blueberry Pistachio Quinoa Parfait with
    Quinoa Praline 158

Spiced Cashew 'Cheesecake' with Red Quinoa Crust 162

ACKNOWLEDGEMENTS

Thank you so much to Carolyn Cope who wrote the fantastic introduction to quinoa (pages 10-19).

Thanks to Abi Waters, Anna Southgate, Rachel Malig and Ann Barrett.

Quantum Books would like to thank the following for supplying images for inclusion in this book:
Shutterstock.com: Iryna Melnyk 8-9, Letterberry 10, Elena Shashkina 11, withGod 12, Anna Hoychuk 18, matka_Wariatka 27, Es75 31, Sea Wave 35, sematadesign 43, Evgeny Karandaev 47, D and J foodstyling 65, Olha Afanasieva 73, Jozef Sowa 85, Piyato 91, sarsmis 95, elena moiseeva 101, Maryna Pleshkun 114, Jiri Hera 125, Vasileios Karafillidis 133, bitt24 145, Magdalena Paluchowska 151, Juan Ci 157, Nickola_Che 160, Olha Afanasieva 169.

While every effort has been made to credit contributors, Quantum Books would like to apologize should there have been any omissions or errors and would be pleased to make the appropriate correction to future editions of the book.